The Spellcaster's Reference

Magickal Timing for the Wheel of the Year

Eileen Holland

WEISERBOOKS
San Francisco, CA / Newburyport, MA

This Book is dedicated to Thoth,
Lord of Books, Reckoner of Time and Seasons.
It is written with heartfelt thanks
to my husband and my son, for everything.

First published in 2009 by
Red Wheel/Weiser, LLC
With offices at:
500 Third Street, Suite 230
San Francisco, CA 94107
www.redwheelweiser.com

ISBN: 978-1-57863-452-1
Library of Congress Cataloging-in-Publication Data is available on request.

Cover and text design by Kathryn Sky-Peck
Typeset in Centaur

Printed in the United States of America
TS
10 9 8 7 6 5 4 3 2 1
Text paper contains a minimum of 30% post-consumer waste material.

Contents

Part IV: Intent and the Wheels of the Year

Introduction

Conventional wisdom informs us that timing is everything. Esoteric philosophy teaches that same truth, but in a deeper and more spiritual way. "Tides of time" is a clichéd phrase, but it is also an accurate one. The heavenly bodies, including the one upon which we stand, move in their courses. Ebb and flow—flux and reflux. The energies stream around us and through us. Nothing stands still except perhaps us, as we pause to contemplate our place in the cosmos. If we are in tune with these energies, we can perceive them. We are then able to notice their effects on us, on others, and on the natural world. If we are adept enough, or possess the requisite knowledge, we can utilize the powerful energies of these tides to empower our magick and rituals.

One of my most cherished childhood possessions was a toy globe. It was just a dented tin thing with bright blue oceans and garishly colored countries, but around its base it had concentric circles that marked the seasons, the houses of the Zodiac, the months, and so on. I spent a lot of time studying that globe and doing what I now know was meditating upon its meaning.

As an adult, I heard the call of the Goddess and began following the Wiccan religion. Wiccans see the year as a wheel, ever turning, and this made perfect sense to me. When Wiccans speak of the Wheel of the Year, we generally mean the solar cycle, the Earth's annual voyage around the Sun, and the eight sabbats with which we celebrate that voyage. The year is actually composed of many interlocking wheels, however. Those who practice magick do well to learn and remember this. All of these cycles influence the natural world, and we can use them to enhance our magick and rituals.

Perhaps it is because of that toy globe that I have always thought of the year as a series of circles. I have always been able to sense our place on the various wheels at any time, and this has been beneficial to me in my practice of magick. It was what prompted me to gather this information, to write this book, and to share my research with you. Please use it constructively, to work positive magick that benefits yourself or others. I am a witch who bides the Rede of "harm none," so any attempt to work negative magick with the aid of this book is more likely to fail than it is to succeed.

PART ONE

Using This Book

T HE OBVIOUS USE FOR *The Spellcaster's Reference* is to determine auspicious times to cast spells, perform rituals, or engage in other magickal operations. It can, however, also be used in many other ways. Perhaps the most important of these is to understand and use the Principle of Correspondences.

Correspondences

"As above, so below."

This basic metaphysical principle means that everything in the Universe is connected, that the macrocosm influences the microcosm. All things and beings share atoms that are in constant motion. Nothing ever actually stands still. Nothing is truly separate or distinct. Everything is connected, but some things are more connected than others.

The Principle of Correspondences is also called the Law of Association. Correspondences are magickal shortcuts, direct links between things. Knowledge of them is extremely useful, because they help to achieve results.

Correspondences are a particular interest of mine, and I have been researching them for a long time. I am fascinated by how they have been applied in so many cultures, faiths, and traditions throughout history. From Mesopotamia to China, from Nabatea to Ireland, and from India to the New World, we find magickal correspondences. There is often wide agreement, but with variations for local climate, fauna, and flora. Sometimes there are cultural or religious differences. Whatever the case, all correspondences are powerful, and you can make use of them to increase the effectiveness of your workings.

Here, we will briefly discuss ways to incorporate correspondences.

Planets

In classical correspondences "planets" mean the seven heavenly bodies that our ancestors could observe with the naked eye: Jupiter, Mars, Mercury, Saturn, Venus, the Moon, and the Sun. The remote planets and even major asteroids also affect everything with their vibrations, but here we will confine ourselves to those heavenly bodies about which the most lore has been accumulated.

Knowing which planet has dominion over a time period or an intent affords the opportunity to utilize that planet's correspondences in a working (see Hours, p. 102). It can help in deciding things such as which angels to evoke for a ritual, what flowers to use, or appropriate items to add to a spell bottle.

Elements

The elements recognized by most traditions are are Earth, Air, Fire, and Water. As with the planets, knowing which elements have dominion over particular intentions or time periods affords the opportunity to utilize their correspondences in workings. Here are some basic examples:

Earth

Color: black, brown, green, ocher, russet

Tool: beeswax candle, pentacle

Charm: clay, honey, mud, musk, pottery, soil, yellow square

Stone: all

Animal: bison, buffalo, cattle, earthworm, goat, jaguar, mole, stag, tortoise, wolf, all burrowing creatures

Metal: coal, lead, mercury ☠

Fungus: mushroom

Incense: amber, benzoin, musk, patchouli, sage, sandalwood

Plant: all, but especially grain, roots, banyan tree, all root vegetables

Goddess: Bona Dea, Ceres (Mother of Corn), Cerridwen, Coatlicue, Danu, Demeter (Queen of the Fruitful Earth), Gaia, Hebat, Isis (Lady of the Land, Queen of the Solid Earth, Goddess of Green Things), Ki, Nerthus, Ninhursag (Lady of the Stone Ground), Nokomis, Onatha, Ops, Parvati (Lady of the Mountain), Persephone, Pomona, Rhea, Sita, Terra Mater (Mother Earth), Tonantzin (Bringer of Maize)

God: Adonis, Arawn, Attis, Bacchus, Cernunnos (Lord of the Forest), the Dagda, Damuzi, Dionysus, Geb, Green Man, Horned God, Marduk (Lord of Growth), Osiris (The Great Green, Grain of the Gods), Pan (Lord of the Woods), Saturn

Evocation: dryads, gnomes, nature spirits, plant devas, Uriel

Air

Color: blue, pale blue, sky blue, clear, white, pastels

Tool: athame, censer, sword, whistle

Charm: bellows, blue circle, fan, feather, flute, perfume

Stone: aventurine, lapis lazuli, clear quartz crystal

Animal: dragon, sphinx, all flying birds and insects

Metal: aluminum, mercury ☠

Fungus: fly agaric ☠, puffball

Incense: all

Plant: almond, angelica, anise, baby's breath, cedar, citronella, all citrus, dandelion, freesia, white geranium, goldenrod, honeysuckle, jasmine, lavender, lemongrass, lilac, pansy, parsley, pennyroyal, snowdrop, thyme, wormwood, yarrow, all plants and trees with spores, aerial roots, fluffy seed heads, winged seed pods, or which provide incense

Goddess: Aditi (Cosmic Space), Aine, Allat, Aradia, Arianrhod, Cardea, Cybele, Freya, Frigg, Hathor (Lady of Heaven), Hera, Iris, Isis (Mistress of the Sky), Juno, Lilith, Mary, Nut, Sekhmet, Semiramis

God: Adad, Amon (The Invisible One), Anu (Expanse of Heaven), Baal (Rider of the Clouds), Boreas, Enlil (Lord of Air), Great Spirit, Horus, Hurukan, Indra (God of the Blue Vault), Jupiter, Kephera, Krishna (Infinite One), Marduk (Wakener of Winds), Mercury, Odin, Quetzalcoatl (Feathered Serpent, Nine Wind), Shiva, Thor, Thoth

Evocation: angels, elves, fairies, Pegasus, Raphael

Fire

Color: gold, orange, hot pink, red, white

Tool: athame, candle, censer, sword

Charm: bonfire, civet, star, red triangle

Stone: coal, flint, hematite, red jasper, lava, obsidian

Animal: dragon, horse, lion, phoenix, salamander, snake

Metal: brass, gold, iron, steel

Incense: brimstone, copal, dragon's blood, frankincense, rose, rosemary

Plant: cactus, carnation, chili pepper, cinnamon, clove, dittany of Crete, eye of Satan ☠, garlic, ginger, High John, horseradish, jalapeño pepper, marigold, mustard, nettle, nutmeg, onion, pepper, radish, rowan, sunflower, tobacco ☠

Goddess: Aetna, Ashtoreth, Ayida Wedo, Bast, Brigid (The Bright One, Lady of the Forge), Chantico (Lady of the Hearth), Coatlicue, Fuji, Graine, Hestia, Kali, Oya, Pelé, Vesta (The Shining One)

God: Agni (Divine Fire), Baal, Belenus (The Brilliant One), Dazhbog, Hephaestus, Lugh (The Shining One), Mithras, Ogun (Lord of Metals), Prometheus, Shango, Tsao Chun (Lord of the Hearth), Vulcan

Evocation: djinna, Michael, Raphael, seraphs, Uriel

Water

Color: aqua, black, blue, clear, green, sea green, ultramarine, white

Tool: bowl, cauldron, chalice

Charm: ambergris, ice, rain, tears, inverted triangle

Stone: blue lace agate, aquamarine, coral, mother-of-pearl, water opal, pearl, clear quartz crystal, river rock, sea salt

Animal: crab, crocodile, dolphin, fish, frog, porpoise, seabirds, diving and wading birds, all marine life

Metal: copper, mercury ☠, silver

Fungus: all

Incense: camphor, coconut, myrrh, strawberry, vanilla

Plant: bat nut, cabbage, calamus, camellia, cantaloupe, cattail, cucumber, driftwood, eryngo, eucalyptus, fern, frangipani, gardenia, kelp, lettuce, lotus, papyrus, rice, rushes, watercress, watermelon, water lily, willow, aromatic rush roots, all gourds, reeds, aquatic plants, succulent plants, and those that grow near water

Goddess: Anahita (Great Goddess of Waters), Atargatis, Benzaiten, Boann, Chalchihuitlcue, Coventina, Danu, Ganga, Ilmatar, Inanna, Luonnotar (The Water Mother), Nantosuelta, Nehalennia (The Seafarer), Oshun, Ran, Sarasvati (Flowing Water), Sulis, Tefnut, Tiamat, Yemaya (Holy Queen Sea)

God: Aegir, Apsu, Dagon, Dylan, Ea (Lord of the House of Water), Enki (God of the Sweet Waters), Hapy, Mannan, Neptune, Njoerd, Poseidon, Tlaloc, Yamm (Prince Sea)

Evocation: Gabriel, Ganymede, merfolk, Michael, nereids, Raphael, water nymphs

✿ Directions

Direction may determine which way you face during a ritual, or while casting a spell. Alternatively, they can help decide things like how to stir a potion, or where to place candles during a working.

✿ Colors

You may incorporate color into a working with your choice of things like fabric for a charm bag, a robe for a ritual, candles for a spell, or an altar cloth for a season.

Numbers

You can incorporate numbers by answering the question "How many?" Examples include how many times you repeat an incantation during a working, how many ingredients you add to a magickal recipe, how many of a deity's titles you use during an invocation, how many candles you place on an altar, how many participants speak during a ritual, or how many knots you tie in a mojo bag.

Metals

You may incorporate metal by your choice of tool for a working—an iron cauldron or a copper wand. You may instead reflect it in altar furnishings like a brass brazier or silver candlesticks. Many different types of objects can be used—copper pennies that you add to a charm bag, or jewelry like a gold necklace or platinum ring that you wear during a ritual.

Stones

You can incorporate a stone by wearing it during a working, such as an amber necklace or a pearl brooch. You may instead place the stone on the altar, using a large crystal, an amethyst sphere, or a dish of turquoise pieces. Small stones can be used in many ways, for instance to encircle candles while spells are cast, or to weave into witch's ladders.

Animals

Real animals, as well as mythical creatures like basilisks and unicorns, are included in this category. The best results are obtained from workings that do not harm animals. Items that have been acquired without causing harm have no negative vibrations that can make your magick go awry. For this reason, images of animals are widely employed instead of actual creatures.

You can wear things like ceramic scarabs and carved stone fetishes on necklaces, for example, or add similar items to medicine pouches. Alternatively, you can place images of creatures—such as wood carvings or clay sculptures—on altars during workings. You can use representations of animals to decorate clothing—for example, a phoenix kimono or a dragon T-shirt that you wear during a working. Magickal tools can also represent animals, like a serpentine wand, or bear images of animals, like a knife with a lion on its handles.

You can also incorporate items provided by animals, such as feathers, into your workings. This means only using things that animals have shed naturally, like fur or snakeskin, or cast off after death, like seashells. You can place shark's teeth or cat hairs into spell bottles, for instance.

☙ Plants

Here are a few examples of the myriad ways that plants can be used magickally. Dried flowers and herbs can be added to wax when candles are made, or ground and added to magickal powders. Fresh flowers can be used to decorate altars and ritual spaces, or woven into chaplets or garlands to wear during workings. Seeds and dried herbs can be added to mojo bags. Wood that is appropriate to a working could be used to kindle a ritual fire for it.

Creativity and imagination are your only limits, except to use common sense. Do not work with plants to which you are allergic. Toxic plants such as henbane or poison hemlock are better avoided. If a plant is illegal where you live, find a magickal substitute for it and use that instead. In this book, poisonous or dangerous substances will be marked with the icon ☠. The best magickal results are generally obtained when a working incorporates only those plants which correspond to its intent, or to its timing.

✤ Fungi

Fungi can be used in the same way as plants. You can add dried mushrooms, for example, to spell bottles and charm bags. You can safely avoid poisonous fungi by only using fungi that are sold as food.

✤ Incense

Burning an appropriate incense can greatly empower a working. You can burn a vanilla joss stick, toss frankincense tears onto a brazier, smolder dragon's blood resin on a charcoal disk, or burn a cone of sandalwood incense or a dried branch of rosemary. The method is not important. What matters is that the incense correspond to the intent or the timing of the ritual, spell, or other magickal working.

✤ Charms

A charm is an object that is incorporated into a working. It can be honey or an egg you eat, milk or wine you drink, ambergris incense you burn, almond oil or musk cologne you use for anointing, a piece of driftwood you add to a fire, a tool you use, or something you wear. A charm may also take the form of an image or an item you place on an altar, at the center of a ritual circle, or elsewhere. I provide a great variety of charms in this book.

✤ Deities

Invocation is an appeal to a higher power. Gods and/or goddesses can be invoked to empower magick. This is especially true when they are specific to a working, or to the auspicious time for it. This book can be used to determine whom it is appropriate to invoke at any given time. When a deity has a relevant title, it is provided in parentheses after his or her name. An example of this is Juno (Light of Heaven), a title for that Roman goddess in her solar aspect.

Invocation may be voiced or psychic, formal or informal—whatever seems correct to you. Remember that it is always polite to show respect and thank deities after you have called upon them.

✎ Evocations

You can also appeal to lesser beings than deities for help in magick and rituals. These include angels, demigods, fairies, heroes, nymphs, and other mythological figures. These beings are *evoked* rather than *invoked*. Simply saying their names aloud and sincerely requesting their assistance is usually sufficient. With this book, you can identify appropriate entities to evoke for workings at specific times.

Rituals and Spells

You can use the information provided here to create spells and rituals, as well as schedule them. Several examples follow. Use them to help create your own magickal workings.

✐ A Ritual for Justice

Let us suppose that you and the members of your metaphysical circle are concerned about justice being done in an impending murder trial. You discuss it and decide to hold a ritual to influence the trial's outcome. Checking Part 4 of this book, *Intent and Magickal Timing*, you discover these correspondences under "Justice":

> Monday/Thursday/Saturday/first hour after sunrise on Sunday, Thursday, or Saturday/first hour after sunset on Sunday, Tuesday, or Wednesday/Waning Moon/Dark Moon/Full Moon in October/October/Libra/Pisces

> *To bring someone to justice*: Saturday/first hour after sunrise on Saturday/first hour after sunset on Tuesday

You are all outraged by the murder, believe that the accused is guilty of it, and want him convicted. The calendar tells you that the Full Moon, one week hence, will fall on a Saturday. It seems clear that holding your ritual at dawn on that Saturday is very auspicious, so that is when you schedule it.

You consult this book's correspondences for Saturday and plan the rite. Everyone agrees to dress in black, wear diamond jewelry, and hold black feathers. You will use seven dark blue pillar candles to delineate the ritual area, each surrounded by a ring of poppy seeds. You will burn frankincense and invoke the Norns.

❧ A Spell to Banish Negativity

Imagine that meditation has helped you to identify a negative pattern that you keep repeating in your life. You are determined to banish this. A friend has given you a Banishing Spell that you think will be good, but you must choose a time to cast it. You check Part 4, and note these correspondences for Banishing:

> Sunset/Saturday/first hour after sunrise on Tuesday or Saturday/first hour after sunset on Tuesday or Friday/Waning Year/Waning Moon/Waning Crescent Moon/Dark Moon/Full Moon in February, September, October, November, or December/Disseminating Moon/Winter/January

It's July, so you are in the Waning Year. The Waning Moon will begin in a few days, so you decide to wait for that. Sunset feels auspicious to you. It is also convenient, so you decide to cast the spell at sunset on your next day off.

As directed by the spell, you gather items that represent the negative pattern and put them on your altar. The spell does not mention other props, so you refer to this book's correspondences for sunset. With their aid, you decide to burn purple candles and jasmine incense while you cast the spell. You also decide to invoke Dusk Zorya and request her help with the banishing.

❧ A Personal Ritual for Strength

Suppose that physical weakness has been a problem for you. You face some upcoming challenges and need to be strong enough to meet them, so you decide to create a personal ritual. You check Part 4, and find these correspondences for Strength:

> Sunday/Tuesday/first hour after sunrise on Sunday or Tuesday/first hour after sunset on Wednesday or Friday/Summer/June/Aries/Taurus/Leo

physical strength: Sunday/Tuesday/first hour after sunrise on Tuesday/first hour after sunset on Friday/Sagittarius

Physical strength is your primary concern. You decide to hold your rite on a Tuesday, and consult an almanac to choose a time that is under the House of Sagittarius. You refer to this book's section on the Zodiac for Sagittarius correspondences, and design your ritual. Four purple candles will mark the quarters. The altar will have a censer of dragon's blood and a large vase of peacock feathers on it. You will wear a purple robe and an amethyst ring. While holding a bow or an arrow, you will invoke Artemis and Apollo, and ask them to send you strength with the speed of an arrow's flight.

⚘ A Ritual for Healing

Imagine that you were injured in an accident. You have had all appropriate medical treatment but want to help your healing go quickly, and go well. You check Part 4, and see these correspondences for Healing:

Dawn/Sunday/Monday/Tuesday/Wednesday/Thursday/Friday/first hour after sunrise on Sunday, Monday, Wednesday, or Friday/first hour after sunset on Monday, Wednesday, Thursday, or Saturday/New Moon/Waxing Moon/Full Moon (especially in February, March, May, August, September, October, November, or December)/Dark Moon/Spring/January/February/June/Gemini/Virgo/Scorpio/Aquarius

to heal wounds: Monday

You have many choices. A large gash in your leg is the injury that worries you the most. Evening is the most convenient time for you to work, so you decide to cast your spell the first hour after sunset on the next Monday.

You decide to make a charm bag, empower it for healing, and carry it until you are fully recovered from the accident. That is when you will enchant it.

Referring to this book's correspondences for Monday, you get a small white muslin bag and add a silver cord as its drawstring. You had already decided to fill the bag with dried healing herbs from your magickal supplies, but now you add some crystal chips, two dimes, and two drops of menstrual blood that your girlfriend has kindly provided.

On that Monday evening, you don a silver ring and a heavy silver bracelet, and prepare your altar. Upon it, you place a pair of pearly white candles in silver candlesticks, a large sphere of clear quartz crystal, and two coconut incense sticks in a holder that is inlaid with mother-of-pearl. At the center of the altar, you make a circle of willow twigs, and you put your charm bag in the middle of that.

You have not written a spell. Instead, you light the incense and candles, call quarters, raise power, and cast a magick circle. You speak sincerely to the Great Mother and ask Her to help you to heal. You hold your charm bag over the incense smoke to suffume it, and empower it with your spell's intent. You promise the Goddess that you will carry the charm bag with you, and sleep with it beside your bed, until your healing is finished. You thank Her, ground power, put the charm bag in your pocket, and clean up. A few weeks later, when you have completely recovered, you dig a hole beneath your favorite tree and bury the charm bag there.

Inspiration & Magickal Things

The Spellcaster's Reference can also be used as a source of inspiration. Here are suggestions for some of the many ways that you can use it. They are merely suggestions, however. You should be creative, and devise your own ways to make ethical use of the information provided in these pages. The information can be used to create many different magickal items. I give you several examples, but please regard them only as guidelines. Use this book to create your own unique amulets, formulas, potions, powders, talismans, and tools.

Francis Barrett wrote in *The Magus* (1801):

> It is here to be particularly noticed by us, that, in forming of a charm, or amulet, it will be of no effect except the very soul of the operator is strongly and intensely exerted and impressed, as it were, and the image of the idea sealed on the charm, or amulet for, without this, in vain will be all the observation of times, hours and constellations therefore, this I have thought fit to mention, once for all, that it may be almost always uppermost in the mind of the operator, for, without this one thing being observed and noticed, any who form seals, &c., do fall short of the wished for effect.

Remember that simply making something at an auspicious time is not enough to imbue it with magick. You must raise power and focus your intent while you make it. The more creativity, ingenuity, intensity, and effort you put into making a magickal object or tool, the more powerful and effective the item is likely to be.

✣ Candles

A stock of candles is a very handy thing for most practitioners of magick to have on hand. Here are two types of candles that you can make.

Daily Solar Cycle Candles

Perhaps it is your practice to pray or make offerings daily, at regular times. If so, you can prepare special candles for that. For instance, you can make pink candles for dawn, and invoke Aurora to empower them. For noon, make bright yellow candles and call upon Ra to charge them. Make purple candles for sunset and invoke the Crone to empower them. For midnight, you can make midnight-blue candles and call upon Hecate to charge them. Finally, for the overnight hours, you can make black candles and invoke Amon to empower them. Alternatively, you can buy candles in those colors and call upon those deities to charge them, as appropriate.

Lunar Cycle Candles

Perhaps you are attuned with the Moon, and generally hold your workings in accord with its cycles. If so, you can use this book to prepare special candles for those workings. For example, you can make silver ones for the New Moon and invoke Selene to enchant them. For the Waxing Crescent Moon, make orange candles, scent them with rose oil, and invoke Tanith or Thoth to empower them. Make red candles for the Waxing Moon and call upon the Maiden to charge them.

For Full Moon workings, make deep-yellow candles, scent them with jasmine oil, and invoke Diana to empower them. Make gray candles for the Waning Moon and call upon Cailleach to enchant them. For the Dark Moon, make black candles and invoke Hecate to empower them. Finally, for a Blue Moon, you can make blue candles. If you prefer, you can also buy a stock of candles in those colors, invoke the appropriate deities to charge them, and use appropriate oils to consecrate them.

Incense

Incense is burned in many traditions, for every kind of working. Incense works best if it is prepared at a time that is auspicious for it, and if it is made with ingredients that correspond to its purpose. Each incense should smell appropriate to the intent of the working, in the opinion of the one who burns it. Scent is very subjective, so experiment to create incense that works for you. If you do not wish to make incense, you can buy sticks or cones of it in specific scents, and use this book's information to empower them at auspicious times for their intended purposes.

Loose incense burns best when its ingredients are powdered, finely crushed or chopped, and well blended. All incense stores best in airtight containers, away from moisture and strong light.

Astrological Incense

Perhaps you often reflect the Zodiac in your workings by casting spells and doing other things at times that are astrologically auspicious for them. If so, you can use this book to make twelve different types of loose incense that can be burned over self-igniting charcoal during workings, as appropriate.

Aries Incense: This may contain equal parts copal, dragon's blood, and myrrh resins, along with cedar chips that have been impregnated with musk oil. It can be made on a Tuesday afternoon after anointing yourself with musk cologne, and invoking Macha or Mars to empower it.

Taurus Incense: This may contain equal parts benzoin resin, dried oakmoss, and patchouli leaves, along with six drops each of hyacinth, rose, and violet oils. It can be blended at midnight on a Friday with a bronze dagger, while wearing green garments and a ring with a green stone. Invoke Frigg or Dionysus to empower it.

Gemini Incense: This may contain equal parts dragon's blood, labdanum, and mastic resins, along with drops of mint oil. It can be made on a breezy Wednesday morning while facing West, mixing it in a container that stands between a pair of stone obelisks. Evoke the Dioscuri to empower it.

Cancer Incense: This may contain equal parts powdered sandalwood, camphor, and myrrh resins, along with drops of ambergris oil. It can be made on a Monday night, while standing in moonlight and wearing something silver. Invoke Diana or Kephera to empower it.

Leo Incense: This may contain equal parts amber chunks, copal and frankincense resins, along with dried saffron threads and drops of civet oil. It can be made on a Sunday morning after anointing yourself with civet oil, while wearing something gold. Invoke Sekhmet or Ra to empower it.

Virgo Incense: This may contain equal parts sandalwood powder, dried patchouli leaves, and cedar chips that have been impregnated with honeysuckle oil. It can be made on a Wednesday night while the Sun or Moon is in Virgo. Invoke Athena or Forseti to empower it.

Libra Incense: This may contain galbanum resin to which drops of apple blossom, rose, and thyme oils have been added. It can be made on a Friday afternoon after anointing with rose oil. Invoke Minerva or Shango to empower it.

Scorpio Incense: This may contain equal parts dried patchouli leaves, benzoin, and myrrh resins, along with drops of pine and violet oils. It can be made on a Tuesday night while the Sun is in the house of Scorpio. Invoke Selqet or Pluto to empower it.

Sagittarius Incense: This may contain equal parts dried copal resin, dried rosemary and sage leaves, along with drops of sweet orange oil. It can be mixed with a peacock feather on a Thursday morning in the Autumn while facing East, wearing purple clothes. Invoke Epona or Jupiter to empower it.

Capricorn Incense: This may contain benzoin resin to which drops of cypress, pine, and spruce oils have been added. It can be made during the Winter, while the Moon is in the house of Capricorn. Invoke Freya or Pan to empower it.

Aquarius Incense: This may contain equal parts benzoin, galbanum, and mastic resins, along with drops of eucalyptus and lavender oils. It can be mixed with a metal wand on a Saturday morning while facing West, wearing blue garments. Evoke Ganymede to empower it.

Pisces Incense: This may contain equal parts dried sage leaves, sandalwood powder, and storax resin, along with drops of ambergris and fish oils. It can be made on a rainy Thursday night while wearing a necklace that has a coral horn on it. Invoke Atargatis or Enki to empower the incense.

Elemental Incense

An Elemental Incense can be used for any working that corresponds to a certain element, or to a time period over which that element has dominion (see Part 2). Here are some examples:

Earth Incense: This may contain equal measures of amber chunks, benzoin resin, dried patchouli leaves, and several drops each of honey and musk oil. It can be mixed atop a pentacle at midnight on a Saturday during the Waxing Moon. Invoke Gaia or the Horned God to empower it.

Air Incense: This may contain equal measures of powdered myrrh resin, sandalwood powder, and cedar wood chips that have been impregnated with lavender oil. It can be blended with a blue feather at dawn on a Wednesday, while wearing blue garments. Evoke Pegasus to empower it.

Fire Incense: This may contain equal measures of copal, dragon's blood, and frankincense resins, along with several drops of rose oil. It can be mixed with an athame at noon on a Sunday during the Summer. Invoke Brigid or Agni to empower it.

Water Incense: This may contain equal measures of powdered camphor and myrrh resin, along with several drops of gardenia oil. It can be mixed in a cauldron during the first hour after sunset on a Monday. Invoke Anahita or Ea to empower it.

ॐ Magickal Oils

Magickal oils are most often used for anointing and consecrating. They can also be added to bathwater, or to magickal recipes such as those for incense and powders. A magickal oil generally contains scented oils that are added to a base oil like olive or mineral oil. Essential oils are natural and the most powerful, but you can also use artificial fragrance oils. The amount of scented oil you add depends on the volume of base oil, and on personal preference. Scent is highly individual. Something that smells beautiful or overwhelming to one person, often elicits a totally different reaction in someone else. You should experiment, and make magickal oils that are pleasing and useful to you.

It is important that an oil's ingredients correspond to its magickal intent, and that the oil be made with that intent firmly in mind. Magickal oils are most effective when they are prepared in this way at a time that is auspicious for their intent, and if a deity who has dominion over the intent or the timing is invoked to empower them.

Number correspondences can be incorporated into the creation of magickal oils in many ways. These may include how many ingredients are used in a formula, or how many charms are placed in a bottle, or how many drops of scented oils are added to the base oil. Substances likes dyes, inks, and food coloring can be used to include color correspondences. These substances often do not mix well with oil, however, so you must shake the bottle well to blend the oil each time it is used. Magickal oils may also contain other ingredients that augment their potency. Small items like seeds or crystal chips can be added to them for this purpose.

It is best to store magickal oils in dark, tightly sealed bottles, in places that are cool, dark, and dry. Shake them to mix before using, and discard them before their base oil's shelf life expires. When an oil's scent is gone, so is its magick.

Here are a few examples of some of the many types of magickal oils you can make with the information in this book. Remember that this is only meant as a guide. You should make oils that please your sense of smell and are appropriate for your workings.

Daily Oils

Some traditions consider the day that corresponds to a person's astrological sign their personal power day. Practitioners who hold this belief often like to work magick on that day. Try making a Personal Power Oil using this book, and use it to anoint yourself or dress candles for workings held on that day. If you burn candles every day, you can use *The Spellcaster's Reference* to help you create a special set of seven oils for consecrating them. Here are some sample recipes:

Sunday Oil: This may contain drops of cinnamon, clove, and bitter orange oils. They can be added to a base of sunflower oil along with drops of tincture of benzoin and yellow food coloring, and a small piece of amber or flakes of gold leaf. It can be mixed on a Sunday at noon while wearing yellow clothes, standing in sunlight, and burning cinnamon incense. Invoke Sunna or Shamash to empower it.

Monday Oil: This may contain drops of jasmine, lavender, and rose oils. They can be added to a base of rice bran oil along with drops of camphor spirit, and flakes of dried coconut and silver leaf. It can be mixed on a Monday night, while standing in moonlight and burning coconut incense. Invoke Luna or Chandra to empower it.

Tuesday Oil: This may contain drops of carnation, cedar, and cinnamon oils. They can be added to a base of mineral oil along with drops of red food coloring, a pine needle, and a small piece of dragon's blood resin. It can be mixed on a Tuesday with a dagger, sword, or athame on the altar, while facing East, burning dragon's blood incense and wearing an iron ring. Invoke the Morrigan or Tyr to empower it.

Wednesday Oil: This may contain drops of bayberry, rosemary, and violet oils. They can be added to a base of hazelnut oil along with a small cinnamon chip, a hematite chip, and some orange glitter. It can be mixed on a Wednesday while wearing blue clothes and burning sage incense. Invoke Ma'at or Odin to empower it.

Thursday Oil: This may contain drops of calendula (marigold), lemon balm, and sage oils. They can be added to a base of olive oil, along with drops of blue food coloring, three rye seeds, and some saffron threads. It can be mixed on a Thursday with a peacock feather, while wearing a crown of laurel (bay) leaves and burning sage incense. Invoking Asase Yaa or Thor to empower it.

Friday Oil: This may contain drops of apple blossom, peppermint, and rose oils. They can be added to a base of almond oil along with drops of pink or green food coloring, a very small piece of copper wire, and five dried coriander seeds or rose hips. It can be mixed at dawn on a Friday with a pigeon feather, while wearing green garments and burning rose incense. Invoke Freya or Freyr to empower it.

Saturday Oil: This may contain drops of basil, hyacinth, and thyme oils. They can be added to a base of sesame oil along with drops of black ink or food coloring, a sliver of pumice stone, and seven poppy seeds. It can be mixed with a black feather on a Saturday while dressed in black, facing North and burning patchouli incense. Invoke Cybele or Ninib to empower it.

Planetary Oils

A Planetary Oil can be used for any working or time period over which a planet has dominion (see page 102). Here is an example of a Planetary Oil for each planet:

Jupiter Oil: A Jupiter Oil may contain drops of cedar, cinnamon, and clove oils. They can be added to a base of olive oil along with a small piece of lapis lazuli, a raw almond, and some blue glitter. It can be mixed on a Thursday during a thunderstorm, while wearing something made of wool and burning vanilla incense. Invoke Hera or Jupiter to empower it.

Mars Oil: A Mars Oil may contain drops of carnation, cedar, and musk oils. They can be added to a base of olive oil along with red coloring, a rose thorn, a few cactus needles, and a coffee bean. It can be mixed with an athame on a Tuesday night while wearing a red garment, facing South, and burning dragon's blood resin. Invoke Sekhmet or Mars to empower it.

Mercury Oil: A Mercury Oil may contain drops of bergamot, mint, and pennyroyal oils. They can be added to a base of hazelnut oil along with two dill seeds, two star anise, and some multicolor glitter. It can be mixed on a breezy Wednesday while facing North and burning sandalwood incense. Invoke Pombagira or Mercury to empower it.

Moon Oil: A Moon Oil may contain drops of gardenia, jasmine, and lemongrass oils. They can be added to a base of mineral oil, along with a drop of spirits of camphor, a tiny white seashell, and a freshwater pearl. It can be mixed on the night of a Full Moon, while wearing a white cotton garment and a silver ring, and burning jasmine incense. Invoke Diana or Sin to empower it, then leave it to stand in moonlight overnight.

Saturn Oil: A Saturn Oil may contain drops of fir, hyacinth, and violet oils. They can be added to a base of mineral oil, along with two caraway seeds, two pomegranate seeds, and a small piece of a black root. It can be mixed on a Saturday afternoon with your left hand while wearing black clothes and burning brimstone. Invoke Kali or Saturn to empower it.

Sun Oil: A Sun Oil may contain drops of cinnamon, lemon, and orange essential oils. They can be added to a base of sunflower oil, along with a drop of honey, yellow coloring, and a tiny chunk of amber. It can be mixed at noon on a sunny Sunday while wearing a gold ring and burning frankincense. Invoke Amaterasu or Phoebus Apollo to empower it, then leave it to stand in bright sunlight for an hour.

Venus Oil: A Venus Oil may contain drops of gardenia, lavender, and rose oils. They can be added to a base of almond oil, along with three coriander seeds, a rose-quartz chip, and some rose hips. It can be mixed at midnight on a Friday while wearing a copper bracelet and burning sweetgrass. Invoke Venus or Angus to empower it.

Mojo Bags

Charm bags, mojo bags, medicine bags—different traditions have different names for them, but they are basically the same thing: small bags, generally with a drawstring closure, that contain charms like herbs and stones, and are empowered with specific magickal intentions. A mojo bag can be for courage, healing, protection, spiritual growth, or any other purpose, but it will work best if it is made at an auspicious time and kept close to the body. For this reason, mojo bags are often worn around the neck, hanging on the chest. This book can help you make many different kinds of mojo bags. Some examples follow:

Love Mojo Bag

Suppose that you want love to enter your life. You refer to the entry for Love and find:

> Dawn/Monday/Thursday/Friday/first hour after sunrise on Monday, Wednesday, or Friday/first hour after sunset on Monday, Thursday, or Saturday/Waxing Year/New Moon/Waxing Moon/Full Moon (especially in March, May, October, and November)/Blue Moon/Summer/April/May/June/October/Taurus/Libra/Capricorn

Many auspicious times are given, but mornings are best for you. You decide to make and consecrate your bag just after dawn on the next Friday, when both the Moon and the Year happen to be waxing.

To your way of thinking, the planet Venus has prime dominion over love, so you decide to incorporate its correspondences into your mojo bag. You fashion it from green fabric, sew it with pink thread, and use a silver cord for its drawstring. Into it, you place three sugar cubes, three cowry shells, three vanilla beans, three rose hips, powdered honey, and dried lavender flowers or rose petals.

You light a pink rose-scented candle and three vanilla joss sticks. Next, you raise power, call quarters, and cast a magick circle. Within it, you close the bag by firmly tying seven knots in its drawstring. You anoint the bag with seven drops of rose oil, and suffume it with the incense and candle smoke by holding it over them. As you do that, you focus on the exact type of love you want to attract, and repeat this incantation seven times:

> *Honey, sugar, vanilla, mead,*
> *Let this charm bring what I need.*

Still holding the mojo bag over the smoke, you invoke the goddess Venus. You speak to her sincerely, tell her what is in your heart, and ask her to empower your mojo bag with sufficient magick to attract it. Finally, you thank her, open the circle, ground the power that you raised, and clean up. You keep the bag close to you for the next few months, occasionally squeezing it as you repeat the incantation, until you meet the type of person that you want to meet. Once that happens, you again thank Venus and bury the mojo bag.

Seasonal Mojo Bags

You can make seasonal mojo bags for yourself, or as gifts for others. Each should be made at an auspicious time, enchanted to attract the specific blessings of that season, kept close at hand throughout the season, and then discarded.

Spring Mojo Bag: For Spring, you may make a green bag and fill it with dried flower petals, feathers from birds that are meaningful to you, and a small image of a dragon. The bag can be made at dawn on the morning of the first New Moon of Spring, and consecrated with rose oil. It may be empowered for awakening, beauty, fertility, growth, and/or renewal. This can be done in the smoke of jasmine incense, while invoking Maia or the Green Man.

Summer Mojo Bag: For Summer, you may make a red bag and fill it with dried carnation petals, sunflower seeds, pearl barley, and a small image of a sphinx. The bag can be made at noon on the first sunny day of Summer, and consecrated with clove oil. It may be empowered for courage, passion, protection, strength, and/or will. This can be done in the smoke of cinnamon incense, while invoking Urania or Khirkhib.

Autumn Mojo Bag: For Autumn, you may make a brown bag and fill it with dried fallen leaves, dried oakmoss and chrysanthemum petals, along with a piece of shed snake skin. The bag can be made in early Autumn, while the Moon is waning, at a time that is ruled by the house of Scorpio, and consecrated with drops of wine. It may be empowered for abundance, lust, maturity, money, transformation, and/or inner work. This can be done in the smoke of patchouli incense, while facing West and invoking Pomona or Tammuz.

Winter Mojo Bag: For Winter, you may make a white bag, draw or embroider snowflakes on it, and fill it with evergreen needles, rosemary, dried holly leaves or berries, and tiny pinecones. The bag can be made at sunset on the first snowy Winter day, and consecrated with melted snow. It may be empowered for banishing, grounding, meditation, dream work, and/or past-life work. This can be done while facing North in the smoke of myrrh incense, while invoking Skadi or Ullr.

Affirmations

An affirmation is a positive statement that you repeat. Affirmations can be used to bolster yourself, improve your mind-set, or modify your behavior. They are powerful tools for positive thinking, tools that can promote positive changes in you and transform your life.

Affirmations are not "one-size-fits-all." We each have different needs and goals, that change as we move through life. It is useful to update your affirmations periodically. Here are some examples of how you can use this book to create personal affirmations for yourself.

✑ Daily Affirmations

The unique energies and correspondences of days can empower affirmations that are used on those days. Whether you need to make something happen, reach a goal, or overcome an obstacle, heartfelt repetitions of the right affirmation on the right day can help you to achieve your objective.

This book can help you to create personal affirmations that are tailored to your needs. One way to do this is to identify what you would like to address. Next, refer to Days of the Week (p. 88). Read through them until you find an auspicious day for your intention, and use that day's correspondences to design your affirmation. Each day is appropriate for many different workings, so you may wish to include more than one thing in your affirmation. Here are some examples.

Sunday Affirmation: "I give myself permission to be happy, and have fun." This can be repeated seven times on Sundays, perhaps while burning cinnamon incense.

Monday Affirmation: "I do not doubt myself." This can be repeated as many times as needed on Mondays, perhaps after anointing yourself with jasmine oil.

Tuesday Affirmation: "I am strong. I can overcome anything." This can be repeated on Tuesdays as many times as needed, perhaps while holding a ceremonial dagger or sword.

Wednesday Affirmation: "I am intelligent and resourceful. I communicate my ideas clearly." This can be repeated five times on Wednesdays, perhaps with one hand on your throat chakra.

Thursday Affirmation: "I notice opportunities, and I act on them." This can be repeated on Thursdays as many times as needed, perhaps while burning sage incense.

Friday Affirmation: "I set things in motion. I can change things." This can be repeated six times on Fridays, perhaps with one hand on your heart chakra.

Saturday Affirmation: "I am wise. I know my limits. I banish the people and things that are toxic to me." This can be repeated six times on Saturdays, perhaps while wearing a diamond ring.

❧ Monthly Affirmations

The specific energies and correspondences of months can also be used to create and empower affirmations. Here are some examples, to use as guidelines for creating monthly affirmations of your own.

January Affirmation: "I have confidence in my goals, and will make them manifest." This can be repeated daily throughout the month as many times as needed, perhaps while holding a pinecone.

February Affirmation: "I clear from my home and my life all that weighs me down, holds me back, serves me ill, or is no longer needed." This can be repeated daily throughout the month, as many times as needed, perhaps while burning sage incense.

March Affirmation: "I am brave. I have the courage to change my life. I can achieve (or maintain) success." This can be repeated daily throughout the month, as many times as needed, perhaps while holding an image of Athena or the Morrigan.

April Affirmation: "I have confidence in myself. I notice opportunities, and take advantage of them." This can be repeated daily throughout the month, as many times as needed, perhaps while holding a hawk feather.

May Affirmation: "I bubble with creative energy. My passion is my strength. I can make things grow, achieve my visions, and inspire others." This can be repeated daily throughout the month, as many times as needed, perhaps after anointing yourself with rose oil.

June Affirmation: "I am strong and responsible. I make good decisions." This can be repeated six times, as often as needed throughout the month, perhaps while holding an image of Isis.

July Affirmation: "I open my arms and accept the blessings that the Universe offers me." This can be repeated daily throughout the month, as many times as needed, perhaps while burning frankincense.

August Affirmation: "I count my blessings, give thanks for them, and appreciate what I have." This can be repeated eight times daily throughout the month, perhaps while holding a sheaf or basket of grain.

September Affirmation: "I think deeply. I am wise. My spirituality grows and deepens." This can be repeated daily throughout the month, as many times as needed, perhaps while burning copal incense.

October Affirmation: "I am hopeful about the future. I release all my anger, resentments, hard feelings, and everything that limits me or holds me back." This can be repeated daily throughout the month, as many times as needed, perhaps while holding newly fallen leaves.

November Affirmation: "I am brave and flexible. I call upon my ancestors to guide me, as I prepare for my future." This can be repeated daily as many times as needed throughout the month, perhaps while holding something that represents your ancestors or their culture.

December Affirmation: "I give myself permission to emerge, and to shine." This can be repeated daily throughout the month, as many times as needed, perhaps while burning myrrh incense.

✒ Seasonal Affirmations

Each season has specific energy that makes it auspicious for certain workings. You can use this book to access seasonal energy and correspondences in order to create many different affirmations. Examples follow, as guidelines.

Spring Affirmation: "I awaken. I am reborn. I am beautiful (or handsome). I feel alive. I grow and I thrive." This can be repeated daily during the Spring, as many times as needed, perhaps after anointing yourself with a floral cologne, perfume, or oil.

Summer Affirmation: "I am brave and passionate. I have infinite capacity for love. I wield the magickal energy that flows through me." This can be repeated daily during the Summer, as many times as needed, perhaps while burning ginger incense.

Autumn Affirmation: "I deserve abundance. I deserve abundance. I am ready to harvest all the seeds that I have sown." This can be repeated daily throughout the Autumn, as many times as needed, perhaps while holding a chalice of water.

Winter Affirmation: "I am grounded. My feet are planted firmly. I build solid foundations for myself. I have vast inner resources, and can find my answers within." This can be repeated daily during the Winter, as many times as needed, perhaps while holding an evergreen branch.

✑ Yearly Affirmations

The energies and correspondences of the two halves of the year are distinctly different—directly opposite, in many cases. You can use them to create powerful personal affirmations that address a wide variety of things. Examples are provided, as guidelines.

Waxing Year Affirmation: "I attract positive people and situations. I can overcome obstacles. I strengthen the relationships that are important to me. I invite positive changes in my circumstances." This can be repeated daily from Winter Solstice to Summer Solstice, as many times as needed, perhaps while wearing a crown of oak leaves.

Waning Year Affirmation: "I banish from my life all that is baneful to me. I will end my bad habits. I avert everything with negative energy. I keep clear my home and my life, so that I may thrive." This can be repeated daily from Summer Solstice to Winter Solstice, as many times as needed, perhaps while holding or regarding an image of the Horned God.

Guidance

The Spellcaster's Reference can also be used for guidance. Pinpoint your position on the Wheel of the Year, and open to that page. Ask your question, something like:

Where should my focus be?

What should I work on?

Why aren't I content?

What is the source of my problem?

How can I change things?

What am I missing?

What is my purpose in life?

How can I improve things?

Read the entry with an open, unfocused mind, and your answer should jump out at you. Nothing jumps? You've selected the wrong Wheel. Try another, such as the day or the season, and you should find your answer there.

Suppose that you ask how you can improve your life and choose the current lunar phase, which is Full Moon. You scan the entry and "dream work" jumps out at you. Thinking about it, you realize that you have not been sleeping well, or paying attention to your dreams. You resolve to improve your sleep habits, to actually block out eight hours for rest every night. You also buy a notebook, write Dream Journal on its cover, and place it beside your bed with a pen. By doing this, you have made arrangements to contact your subconscious and see what messages it may have for you. In a few weeks, when you see whether or not dream work and better sleep have improved the quality of your life, you will know if this was the answer you sought.

Now suppose that you ask what you should work on, and choose the current astrological phase, which is Pisces. You scan that entry and "reorganization" jumps out at you. That is obvious, as you sit at an untidy desk in a messy room. You realize that you can get your life in order by getting your files and finances in order. This is something that has been simmering at the back of your mind for some time, but now you're actually ready to do it.

Now imagine asking the same question—"What should I work on?"—but choose the Wheel for the day of the week. When you scan that entry, "personal fulfillment" jumps out at you. It doesn't make immediate sense to you why that should resonate so strongly, so you meditate on it. You are surprised when you realize that you have been putting others ahead of yourself for many years, and that this has left you with unfulfilled goals and dreams. You discover that better time-management may allow you to work on the most important of your goals, while still helping others.

Global Use of This Book

I live in the Northern Hemisphere. I write from that perspective, but *The Spellcaster's Reference* can be used anywhere on this planet. Much of it can be used as written because the days, planetary hours, astrological year, and lunar phases influence magick the same way everywhere on Earth.

Certain parts of the book will need to be adapted or disregarded in some places. For example, there are locations near the poles where the Sun never sets, or never rises. The daily solar cycle information will need to be adjusted or ignored as seems best to practitioners living there. Many places do not experience four traditional seasons, so the same will need to be done with the seasonal information in those locales. That was how I practiced when I lived in Egypt, utilizing the summer information much of the year, but making scant use of other seasonal correspondences.

Many things in the Southern Hemisphere occur in an opposite way to those in the Northern Hemisphere. I've never been there, but practitioners in places like Australia, New Zealand and South America have told me how they work. These suggestions are based on that. Reverse the information about the months, to match the seasons as they occur: apply January's information to June, February's to July, and so on. Do the same with each month's Full Moon. Use information about the halves of the year when they happen: Waning Year from Winter Solstice to Summer Solstice, and Waxing Year from Summer Solstice to Winter Solstice.

Northern Hemisphere authors have written most works about magick. That is reflected in the correspondences found herein, but they are not the only ones. Mother Nature provides us with everything we need to work magick, provides it abundantly and in great diversity. Adjust the correspondences as needed, to reflect climate or other conditions, and incorporate local things. Be sensitive to your surroundings, and notice the effects of the Wheels of the Year on the natural world. There is magick in everything, from flora to fauna to the different types of sand and snow.

This book is best used in accord with personal practices or traditions, and local conditions. I have a great imagination, but I cannot truly know what the flow of energy feels like near the equator or in the Southern Hemisphere. I hope that all readers will trust their inner voices, harm none, and use this book in the ways that seem best to them. Adopt whatever works, and adapt or bypass the rest.

Glossary

I have drawn on widely varied sources, including ancient ones to create *The Spellcaster's Reference.* Because some of the words in this book may be unfamiliar to you, I have included an extensive Glossary at the end of the book.

Since plants often have a multitude of folk names, I have also provided a reference of the botanical names for the most unusual plants, along with many of their alternate folk names.

PART TWO

The Year

EVISING WAYS TO MEASURE TIME is one of the things that defines us as human. At our least sophisticated, before we learned to write, we cut notches on sticks or made marks on cave walls to count the passages of the Moon. Different cultures eventually created various systems of time measurement and produced different calendars, many of which were repeatedly revised because they were unwieldy or simply didn't work.

Terrans finally settled on our present system of 365 days, divided into twelve months, with seven-day weeks composed of 24-hour days. We can utilize the various divisions of that calendar year in our magick and rituals.

Waxing Year, Waning Year

The most basic of the Wheels of the Year is the solar cycle that bisects the year at the solstices, into its waxing and waning halves. Sunlight increases from Winter Solstice to Summer Solstice, then decreases from Summer Solstice to Winter Solstice.

Waxing Year

The Waxing Year begins at Winter Solstice, when the Sun is least able to warm the Earth. The Sun is then "reborn." The light half of the year begins, and the hours of daylight start to lengthen. The dark or waning half of the year begins at Summer Solstice with the longest day; the waxing half of the year begins with the longest night.

In Wiccan terms, this is when the Child of Promise is reborn to the Mother Goddess. In mythological terms, tanists exchange places: Dionysus gives way to Apollo, Set to Osiris, Mot to Baal, John the Baptist to Jesus, the Holly King to the Oak King, the Green Knight to Sir Gawain, and so on. The rule of the Lord of Light supersedes that of the Dark Lord over the Wheel of the Year. Balance is maintained.

This half of the year, like the Waxing Moon and the Rising Sun, is a powerful time for deosil magick. It is a great time for constructive workings that attract, charge, improve, increase, invite, strengthen, and overcome. Examples are workings to attract love, charge magickal tools, improve living standards, increase income, invite success, strengthen relationships, and overcome darkness. It is also an auspicious time for workings that are related to light, manhood, masculinity, and warmth.

Waxing Year Correspondences

Sun/Male

Animal: ram, robin

Plant: mistletoe, oak

God: Adonis, Apollo, Baal, Byelobog, Green Man, Jesus, Lugh, Osiris

Evocation: Achilles, Diarmuid, Hercules, Oak King, Robin Redbreast, Robin Redman (King of the Waxing Year), Sir Gawain

✍ Waning Year

The Waning Year begins at Summer Solstice, when the Sun "dies" and the hours of daylight begin to shorten. Summer Solstice marks the peak power of the Sun. Just as the light or waxing half of the year began at Winter Solstice with the longest night, the dark or waning half begins now at Summer Solstice with the longest day.

In Wiccan terms, the God stands in virile manhood beside the pregnant Goddess, and lovingly offers himself in sacrifice for the good of all. In mythological terms, tanists exchange places: Apollo gives way to Dionysus, Diarmuid to Finn Mac Cool, Lugh to Bran, Byelobog to Czarnobog, Robin Redbreast to Jenny Wren, Achilles to Agamemnon, and so on. The rule of the Dark Lord supersedes that of the Lord of Light over the Wheel of the Year. Balance is maintained.

This half of the year, like the Waning Moon and the Setting Sun, is a powerful time for widdershins magick. It is a great time for workings that avert, banish, clear, decrease, end, lessen, repel, and weaken. Examples include workings to avert evil, banish bad habits, clear entities, decrease loneliness, end illness, lessen financial problems, repel enemies, and weaken negative influences. It is also an auspicious time for workings that are related to darkness, femininity, and womanliness.

Waning Year Correspondences
Sun/Female

Animal: wren

Plant: holly, ivy

God: Balor, Beli, Bran, Czarnobog, Dionysus, Horned God, Mot, Set

Evocation: Agamemnon, Finn Mac Cool, Green Knight, Holly King, Jenny Wren, John the Baptist, Tityas

The Seasons

The seasons, which divide the year by four, are profound sources of magick. They constantly change, so their energy is a powerful force for making things happen.

Seasonal Correspondences

Sun/Earth/Wednesday/Spring/Summer/Autumn/Winter

Number: 4

Goddess: Brigantia, Brigid, Cailleach, Estsanatlehi, Hera, the Horai (the Hours), Ninhursag, Rhea, Tamar, Tara, Themis

Goddess for the change of the seasons: Isis, Al Uzza, Yolkai Estsan (White Shell Woman)

Goddess to regulate the seasons: the Horai

Goddess for seasonal magick: Aestas, Anieros, Axiocersa, Beiwe, Brigid, Cailleach, Lassair, Rhea, Summer Daughter, Tamar, Themis, Al-Uzzah

God: Baal, the Bacabs (Lords of the Seasons), the Dagda, Dazhbog, Hermes, Kusor, Mercury, Thoth (Reckoner of Time and Seasons)

God for the change of seasons: the Dagda, Mithras, Tate, Vertumnus (the Changer)

Spring

Spring is a powerful time for visualization, dragon magick, flower magick, garden magick, Air magick/rituals/spells, and workings that are related to awakening, beauty, beginning, birth, calm, fertility, gentleness, growth, healing, increase, innocence, laughter, purification, rebirth, renewal, rejuvenation, youth, cyclical rebeginning, new growth, nourishing rain, psychic awareness, the life force, and the renewal of Nature. It is also an auspicious time to awaken fertility, edit possessions, renew vitality, plant magickal gardens, and awaken anything that has been dormant.

Spring Correspondences

Sunrise/New Moon/Waxing Moon/Air/East/Aries/Gemini/Taurus

Color: green, spring green, all pastels

Stone: emerald

Charm: maiden, tree

Plant: daffodil, dogwood, hyacinth, iris, lilac, lily, peony, tulip, all Spring flowers, and the plants that bloom, ripen, or are otherwise prominent during this season in your area

Incense: jasmine, rose, all floral scents

Animal: dragon, lamb, lion, ram, robin, all birds, and the animals that are most active during this season where you live

Goddess: Aega, Anna Perenna, Anthea, Aphrodite Antheia (Aphrodite of the Flowers), Aphrodite Camaetho, Artemis, Beiwe, Blodeuwedd (Flower Bride), Britomartis, Chloris, Creiddylad (May Queen), Cunneware, Dictynna, Eunomia, Feronia, Flora, Freya, Frigg, Goda (The Good), Holda, Idunn, Inghean Bhuidhe (Yellow-haired Girl), Kore (the Maiden), Lada, Ma-Ku, Maeve, Maia, the Maiden, Olwen (May Queen), Ostara, Persephone, Phyllis, Prosperine, Rana Nedia, Renpet, Rhea, Sita, T'ao Hua Hsiennui (Peach Blossom Girl), Venus, Vesna, the White Goddess, Xochiquetzal, Yaya-Zakurai

God: Adonis, Aleion, Ares, Attis, Atunis, Baal, Bran, Damuzi, Dionysus Antheus, Enlil, Green Man, Jarillo (Young Lord), Jarovit, Kokopelli, Kostrubonko, Krishna Mahadeva, Kuan Kung, Kuan Ti, Llew Llaw, Marduk, Mars, Ningirsu, Ninurta, Patrimpas, Red Tezcatlipoca, Tammuz, Tsai Shen, the Usins, Vishnu, Xipe Totec (Lord of Spring), Zeus

Evocation: Amatiel, Caracasa, Commissoros, Core, Guinevere, Hyacinthus, Milkiel, Narcissus, nymphs, Penelopeia

✺ Summer

Summer is a powerful time for vision quests, Fire magick/rituals/spells, and workings that are related to courage, friendship, love, marriage, passion, protection, strength, warmth, will, yang, magickal energy, mature vigor, and nourishing dew.

Summer Correspondences

Noon/Sun/Full Moon/Fire/South/Male/Cancer/Leo/Virgo

Color: red, orange, yellow

Stone: lapis lazuli, ruby, sunstone

Charm: honey

Plant: carnation, grain, sunflower, and the plants that bloom, ripen, or are otherwise prominent during this season in your area

Incense: cinnamon, clove, ginger

Animal: bee, eagle, goat, lion, sphinx, and the animals that are most active during this season where you live

Goddess: Aibheaeg, Aine, Aphrodite Camaetho, Artemis, Auxo, Brigid, Danu, Demeter, Ebhlinne, Eirene, Grismadevi, Hiribi, the Mother, Olwen, Persephone, Sekhmet, Summer Daughter, Urania (Queen of Summer), Venus Urania

God: Adonis, Apollo, Ares, Attis, Havgan (Summer Song), Helios, Khirkhib (King of Summer), Kuan Kung, Kuan Ti, Lugh, Marduk, Mars, Ninib, Porevit, Ra, Rapiu, Tammuz, Zeus

Evocation: Gargatel, Gaviel, nymphs, Tariel, Tubiel, Uriel

 # Autumn

Autumn is a powerful time for scrying, Crone magick, inner work, trance magick, Water magick/rituals/spells, and workings that are related to abundance, battle, death, employment, gathering, harvest, hunting, lust, maturity, money, sorrow, transformation, and new possessions.

Autumn Correspondences

Waning Moon/Water/West/Libra/Sagittarius/Scorpio

Color: brown, gold, olive green, maroon, orange, russet, wine

Stone: sapphire

Charm: cauldron, grape juice, wine

Plant: bearberry, chrysanthemum, grapevine, oakmoss, vetiver, white poplar, autumn leaves, and the plants that bloom, ripen, or are otherwise prominent during this season in your area

Incense: copal, patchouli

Animal: hare, lynx, snake, squirrel, tiger, and the animals that are most active during this season where you live

Goddess: Ambika, Anieros, Annapurna, Aphrodite, Aphrodite Camaetho, Athena, Baba Yaga, Ba'u, Brigid, Cailleach, Campestres, Carpo, Ceres, the Crone, Demeter, Diana, Dike, Erce, Feronia, Geshtinanna, Habondia (She of Abundance), Hecate, Hera, Latiaran, Mama Allpa, Marzana,

Modron, Morgay, Pachamama, Pomona, Rugiu Boba, Saraddevi, Sif, Tail-tiu, Tatsuta-Hime, Vacuna, Xi Wang Mu, Zisa

God: Adad (Lord of Abundance), Baal, Chang Fei, Dionysus, Dionysus Ignigema, Dionysus Pyrigenes, Horned God, Khirkhib (King of the Raiding Season), Phanes, Ruevit, Svantovit, Tammuz, Torquaret

Evocation: Guabarel, Michael, sylphs, Tarquam

🌿 Winter

Winter is a powerful time for banishing, grounding, meditation, Crone magick, dream magick, dream work, ice magick, inner work, snow magick, past-life work, Earth magick/rituals/spells, and for workings that are related to dormancy, endings, darkness, death, dreams, silence, sleep, sorrow, and yin. This is also an auspicious time to find answers within.

Winter Correspondences

Sunset/Waning Moon/Dark Moon/Earth/Water/North/Female/Aquarius/Capricorn/Pisces

Color: black, pale blue, gray, white

Stone: diamond, snowflake obsidian

Plant: evergreens, fir, holly, pine, spruce, rosemary, wintergreen, and the plants that bloom, ripen, or are otherwise prominent during this season in your area

Incense: benzoin, frankincense, myrrh, pine resin, rosemary

Animal: ox, fish, penguin, polar bear, reindeer, snake, tortoise, and the animals that are most active during this season where you live

Goddess: Angerboda (Frost Giantess), Annis (The Blue Hag), Athena, Brigid, Cailleach (Winter Hag), Cerridwen (White Lady of Death), the Crone, Ereshkigal, the Fates, the Furies, the Graces, Hemantadevi, Holda (White Lady), Juno Februa, Marzana, Möüll, Perchta (Yuletide Witch), Skadi (Snowshoe Goddess), Thorri (Spirit of Winter), Yuki-Onne (Snow Maiden)

God: Adad, Arawn, Baal Shamin, Boreas, Chang Fei, Cronos, Dionysus, Enten, Februus, Hades, Hoder, Horned God (Lord of Winter), Khuno, Morning Star, Pluto, Seker, Svarozhich, Tsa'qamae (Head Winter Dancer), Ullr, Zeus

Evocation: Attarib, Cetarari, Gabriel, Jack Frost, Old Man Winter, the Snow Queen, Thorri, Windigo

Months

The months divide the year by twelve. They are sacred to Ninti, Queen of Months, and to Savasi, Mother of the Months. Each one has its own energy, which can be tapped into to boost magickal power.

January

January is a powerful month for inner work, weather divination, wish magick, and workings that are related to abilities, beginnings, conception, confidence, conservation, constancy, goals, healing, organization, patience, precaution, protection, quiet, reversal, safety, and the future. This is also an auspicious time to change course, make plans, take stock, release the past, work on goals, be honest with yourself, meditate on the lessons of the previous calendar year, and banish its negativity.

January Correspondences

Winter/Capricorn/Aquarius

Color: black, blue-violet, dark red, bright white

Number: I

Stone: amber, amazonite, beryl, chrysoprase, garnet, hematite, jacinth, jet, onyx, rubellite

Animal: blue jay, coyote, duck, fox, goose, pheasant, wolf

Plant: alder, birch, carnation, crocus, holy thistle, marjoram, nuts, pinecone, snowdrop

Incense: musk, sandalwood

Goddess: Chang-O, Felicitas, Freya, Hera, Ianuaria, Inanna, Irene, Juno, Juno Antevorta, Juno Postvorta, Pax, Sarasvati, Venus

God: Antu, Great Spirit, Janus

Evocation: Bahman, brownies, Cambiel, Gabriel, gnomes

✿ February

February is a powerful month for clearing and for workings that are related to dormancy, fertility, forgiveness, grace, growth, healing, initiation, inspiration, motivation, openness, passage, patience, peace, preparation, protection, purification, receptivity, respite, sanctuary, sincerity, storms, solitude, emotional release, inner vision, new experiences, spiritual purification, and temporary positions. It is also an auspicious time to banish Winter, dedicate yourself, finish projects, honor ancestors, make plans, look for signs, and meditate on the power of light to overcome darkness, the power of positive energy to overcome negative energy, and the power of goodness to overcome evil.

February Correspondences

Winter/Aquarius/Pisces

Color: light blue, sea-green, purple, violet

Number: 2

Stone: amethyst, aquamarine, beryl, jacinth, jade, jasper, opal, pearl, clear quartz crystal

Animal: chickadee, duck, eagle, otter, raccoon, snipe, wolf

Plant: alder, ash, balm of Gilead, cedar, hyssop, laurel, primrose, rowan, sage, spikenard, violet, willow

Incense: cedar, myrrh, sage

Goddess: Aphrodite, Atargatis, Brigid, Demeter, Diana, Juno, Juno Februa, Kore, the Maiden, Persephone, Prosperine

God: Dis Pater, Februus, Pluto, Quirinus

Evocation: Barbiel, Barchiel, domestic fairies, house-plant devas, Isfandarmend

✖ March

March is a powerful month for vision quests and for workings that are related to achievement, beginnings, change, courage, energy, exploration, ideas, growth, prosperity, renewal, stamina, success, transition, and visions. It is also an auspicious time to begin projects, break illusions, call storms, launch dreams, overcome barriers, balance light and darkness, and see things as they really are.

March Correspondences
Winter/Spring/Pisces/Aries

Color: light blue, pale green, reddish-violet

Number: 3

Stone: amethyst, aquamarine, bloodstone, carnelian, diamond, jasper, opal, ruby, sard, blue topaz

Animal: boar, cougar, crow, fish, hedgehog, lamb, lion, sea crow, sea eagle, worm

Plant: alder, ash, broom, daffodil, yellow dock, dogwood, High John, honeysuckle, Irish moss, jonquil, sugar maple, violet, willow, wood betony

Goddess: Anath, Anna Perenna, Artemis, Astarte, Athena, Bellona, Cybele, Hecate, Holda, Isis, Luna, Minerva, the Morrigan, Ostara

God: Ares, the Green Man, Mars, Teutates, Tyr

Evocation: Machidiel, merfolk, storm spirits

April

April is a powerful month for workings that are related to awakening, change, creation, fertility, growth, longevity, love, novelty, productivity, purity, rebirth, selfishness, self-confidence, self-reliance, vulnerability, anger management, good luck, new beginnings, new directions, and new life. This is also an auspicious time to test yourself, enrich your life, look for openings, meet new people, try something new, and take advantage of opportunities.

April Correspondences
Spring/Aries/Taurus

Color: clear, crimson, gold

Number: 4

Stone: beryl, chrysolite, diamond, garnet, meteorite, peridot, ruby, sapphire, sard, topaz, zircon

Animal: bear, frog, goose, hare, hawk, magpie, rabbit, shad, wildcat, wolf

Plant: alder, basil, bergamot, chive, daisy, geranium, grass, hawthorn, hazel, laurel, moss pink, peony, pine, sweet pea, thistle, all wildflowers, and everything that is in bloom where you live

Incense: dragon's blood, patchouli, pine, all florals

Goddess: Anahita, Aphrodite, Artemis, Astarte, Bast, Ceres, Cybele, Demeter, Flora, Hathor, Ishtar, Kali, Ostara, Persephone, Prosperine, Terra, Venus

God: Angus, Jarillo, Mars

Evocation: Buddha, plant devas

 # May

May is a powerful time for fairy magick, flower magick, garden magick, and workings that are related to attraction, creativity, development, discovery, fertility, growth, happiness, hope, imagination, inspiration, intuition, joy, love, maturity, passion, propagation, protection, resurrection, sex, creative energy, deep longings, hidden promise, inner vision, and sexual freedom. It is also an auspicious time to explore and to attempt new things.

May Correspondences

Spring/Taurus/Gemini

Color: brown, green, emerald green, jade green, pink

Number: 5

Stone: agate, amber, carbuncle, carnelian, chalcedony, emerald, garnet, lapis lazuli, malachite, rose quartz, ruby, tourmaline

Animal: cat, dove, dragon, frog, hare, leopard, lynx, panther, pony, swallow, swan, pairs of animals

Plant: dittany of Crete, elder, foxglove, grass, hawthorn, lily of the valley, mint, mugwort, oak, rose, rowan, thyme, willow, yarrow, May flowers, and everything that is in bloom where you live

Incense: benzoin, myrrh, rose, sandalwood, all florals

Goddess: Aphrodite, Artemis, Bast, Bona Dea, Diana, Maeve (Queen of Beltane), Maia, Mother Earth, Rauni, Venus

God: The Green Man, Horus, Pan

Evocation: Ambriel, elves, fairies, Khurdad, Robin Goodfellow

June

June is a powerful month for fairy magick and for workings that are related to change, commitment, communication, concentration, friendship, health, imagination, innocence, love, marriage, nurture, prevention, protection, purity, responsibility, steadfastness, strength, transition, and family ties. It is also an auspicious time to flourish, avert negative energy, balance inconsistencies, grow strong, maintain course, make decisions, renew dedications, sustain enthusiasm, and take a break.

June Correspondences

Spring/Summer/Gemini/Cancer

Color: bronze, cream, orange

Number: 6

Stone: agate, alexandrite, amber, chalcedony, chrysoprase, citrine, emerald, fluorite, moonstone, opal, pearl, ruby, tiger's-eye, topaz, turquoise, tourmaline

Animal: bear, butterfly, frog, horse, monkey, peacock, toad, wren

Plant: corn, couch grass, hawthorn, hay, holly, lavender, lotus, meadowsweet, moss, oak, oakmoss, orchid, parsley, rose, scullcap, strawberry, tansy, vervain, yarrow, June flowers, ripe berries, and everything that is in bloom where you live

Incense: lavender, rose

Goddess: Aine, Bendis, Cerridwen, Hera, Ishtar, Isis, Juno, Neith, Uni

God: The Green Man

Evocation: elves, fairies, Muriel, sylphs

❧ July

July is a powerful month for divination, meditation, dream work, lunar magick, psychic work, and workings that are related to authority, blessings, contentment, fun, fulfillment, joy, leisure, potency, preparation, success, vitality, and spiritual goals. It is also an auspicious time to clear negativity, replenish energy, tend projects, and open your third eye.

July Correspondences
Summer/Cancer/Leo

Color: bluish-gray, red, silver

Number: 7

Stone: white agate, carnelian, lapis lazuli, moonstone, onyx, pearl, peridot, rubellite, ruby, sapphire, sardonyx, turquoise

Animal: buck, crab, crane, dolphin, ibis, mosquito, starling, swallow, turtle, whale

Plant: acacia, agrimony, ash, lemon balm, corn, grain, hay, hazel, holly, honeysuckle, hyssop, jasmine, lotus, oak, orris root, rose, water lily

Incense: frankincense, jasmine

Goddess: Athena, Cerridwen, Hel, Holda, Ishtar, Juno, Nephthys, Opet, Sekhmet, Sothis, Spider Woman, Venus

God: Jupiter, Kephera

Evocation: brownies, corn spirits, Verchiel

August

August is a powerful month for meditation, herbal magick, and workings that are related to courage, determination, fidelity, fortitude, friendship, gathering, harvesting, health, peace, perseverance, protection, stamina, symmetry, and vitality. It is also an auspicious time to take stock, count your blessings, appreciate what you have, and bring things to fruition.

August Correspondences
Summer/Leo/Virgo

Color: gold, light green, yellow

Number: 8

Stone: fire agate, alexandrite, amethyst, carnelian, diamond, emerald, jasper, moonstone, onyx, peridot, pyrite, ruby, sard, sardonyx, tiger's-eye, topaz, tourmaline

Animal: crane, dragon, eagle, falcon, lion, phoenix, sphinx, sturgeon

Plant: alder, angelica, barley, cedar, chamomile, corn, gladiola, grapevine, hazel, heliotrope, holly, St. John's wort, sunflower, and every type of fruit, grain, and herb that ripens at this time in your area

Incense: cedar, frankincense

Goddess: Ceres, Demeter, Diana, Hathor, Hecate, Nemesis

God: Ganesha, Lugh, Thoth

Evocation: corn spirits, dryads, Hamaliel, Shahrivari

⚜ September

September is a powerful month for clearing, inner work, and workings that are related to change, closure, culmination, fulfillment, harvest, intuition, organization, repentance, transition, wisdom, deep thought, good fortune, and spiritual growth. It is also an auspicious time to conclude projects, finish matters, and clear backlogs and blockages that prevent progress.

September Correspondences

Autumn/Summer/Virgo/Libra

Color: deep blue, brown, chartreuse, yellow

Number: 9

Stone: chrysolite, citrine, olivine, peridot, sapphire, sardonyx, blue tourmaline

Animal: calf, deer, ibis, jackal, snake, sparrow, sturgeon

Plant: aster, barley, beans, bergamot, chrysanthemum, corn, fennel, grapevine, hazel, ivy, larch, laurel, mulberry, nuts, pumpkin, rye, scullcap, squash, valerian, wheat, wild rice, and every type of food plant that ripens at this time in your area

Incense: copal, mastic, storax

Goddess: Ceres, Chang-O, Demeter, Freya, the Great Mother, Isis, Nephthys, Persephone

God: Jupiter, Thor, Thoth, Vulcan

Evocation: trooping fairies, Mihr, Uriel, Zuriel

🐚 October

October is a powerful month for releasing, psychic work, spirit work, and workings that are related to balance, consequences, harvest, honesty, hope, hunting, justice, karma, love, objectivity, reincarnation, transformation, and inner harmony. It is also an auspicious time to examine accomplishments, understand yourself, and learn a new method of divination.

October Correspondences
Autumn/Libra/Scorpio

Color: multi-colors, deep turquoise

Number: I

Stone: agate, aquamarine, beryl, garnet, opal, sapphire, tourmaline, pink tourmaline, turquoise

Animal: beaver, boar, crow, deer, elephant, heron, jackal, ram, scorpion, stag

Plant: acacia, angelica, blackberry, burdock, calendula, catnip, cosmos, cypress, dahlia, grapevine, ivy, marigold, pennyroyal, reed, senna, thyme, uva ursi, yew, and all trees with falling leaves

Goddess: Astarte, Belili, the Crone, Demeter, Hathor, Hecate

God: Cernunnos, the Horned God, Mars, Osiris

Evocation: Aban, banshees, Barbiel, corn spirits

November

November is a powerful month for invocation, releasing, spirit communication, and for workings that are related to ancestors, courage, empathy, flexibility, hunting, preparation, prophecy, remembering, sacrifice, transformation, understanding, and good fortune. It is also an auspicious time to work with familiars and animal guides.

November Correspondences
Autumn/Scorpio/Sagittarius

Color: black, gray, sea-green, purple, white, yellow

Number: 2, 11

Stone: amber, amethyst, Apache tear, beryl, chrysoberyl, citrine, jacinth, lapis lazuli, malachite, obsidian, onyx, pearl, tiger's-eye, topaz

Animal: bat, beaver, boar, crocodile, deer, dog, falcon, goose, harrier hawk, horse, jackal, owl, raven, scorpion, sow, snake, sparrow, white stag, wolf

Plant: alder, apple, betony, birch, blessed thistle, borage, cactus, chrysanthemum, cinquefoil, cypress, dahlia, elder, ginger, grains of paradise, hops, hyssop, ivy, mugwort, nutmeg, oak, peppermint, pine, reed, rosemary, sassafras, star anise, verbena, wormwood, yew, and all trees that still have leaves

Incense: cedar, dragon's blood, patchouli, pine, rosemary

Goddess: Astarte, Baba Yaga, Bast, Cailleach, Cerridwen, Circe, Cybele, Diana, Freya, Hathor, Hecate, Hel, Holda, Kali, Mawu, Nephthys, Nicnevin, Sekhmet (Lady of the Messengers of Death), Skadi

God: Crom Cruach (Crooked One of the Mound), the Horned God, Namtar, Osiris, Thanatos, Zeus Maimaktes

Evocation: Adnachiel, ancestors, angels, Azar, banshees, the Maenads, subterranean fairies

❧ December

December is a powerful month for pathworking, inner work, and workings that are related to brotherhood, celebration, change, emergence, endurance, generosity, introspection, joy, kindness, law, rebirth, return, transition, and unselfishness. It is also an auspicious time to let yourself shine.

December Correspondences

Autumn/Winter/Sagittarius/Capricorn

Color: aqua, green, greenish-blue, bright red, turquoise

Number: 3

Stone: aquamarine, beryl, bloodstone, chrysoprase, jacinth, lapis lazuli, malachite, peridot, ruby, serpentine, blue topaz, turquoise, blue zircon

Animal: bear, deer, goat, groundhog, horse, mouse, rook, snowy owl, wolf

Plant: Christmas cactus, elder, fir, holly, English ivy, mistletoe, oak, peach, pine, poinsettia, rose geranium, rowan

Incense: frankincense, myrrh, patchouli, rose, violet

Goddess: Athena, the Fates, Freya, Hathor, Hecate, Ix Chel, Lucina, Minerva, Neith, the Norns, Vesta

God: Attis, Dionysus, Freyr, the Horned God, Odin, Osiris, Poseidon, Saturn

Evocation: Anael, Dai, Haniel, sylvan spirits

The Astrological Year

Just as the annual calendar divides the year into twelve months, the Zodiac divides it into twelve houses. The zodiacal year is believed to have originated in Babylon, evolving from episodes in the *Epic of Gilgamesh.* The ancient stories of Gilgamesh, of Jason and the Argonauts, of the twelve labors of Hercules, and even the passion play of Isis and Osiris, may be read as the voyage of the year through the twelve houses of the Zodiac.

The astrological year begins in the spring with Aries, the Ram, and circles onward to Pisces, the Fish. Starting and ending dates for the various houses and signs are approximate, as you will find slightly different ones in various sources. Each sign runs from the latter part of a calendar month, to the latter part of the next calendar month. If you want to do a working near a cusp—when two signs come near or overlap—you can use correspondences from either of them, or from both.

The Zodiac is sacred to the goddesses Cerridwen, Tanith, and Al Uzza. It has been called Ishtar's Girdle, The Beastiary, the Circle of Animals, the Girdle of Gaia, the Circle of the Sky, and Our Ladye's Way. The bull was originally a cow, the lion a lioness, the ram an ewe, and so on, until patriarchy supplanted matriarchy.

It is important to note that the astrological year is lunar as well as solar. The Sun transits through each of the twelve houses of the Zodiac for one month of the year, while the Moon transits through each house every month. An almanac or an astrological almanac can be used to track this. If, for example, it is July and you want to cast a spell that is best cast under Taurus, you need not wait until April or May of the next year. With the help of an almanac you can determine when the Moon will be in Taurus during July, and cast your spell then.

Aries

March 21 to April 19 or 20

This is a powerful time for Fire magick/rituals/spells and workings that are related to action, activity, ambition, anger, appearance, assertiveness, authority, battle, beginning(s), birth, boldness, charisma, childishness, competition, confidence, courage, decisiveness, disharmony, energy, enterprise, exploration, fearlessness, force, growth, idealism, impatience, impulsiveness, independence, initiative, jealousy, jobs, leadership, need, novelty, optimism, passion, quarrels, rebirth, self-awareness, self-control, self-esteem, selfishness, spontaneity, strength, tools, urgency, violence, willpower, yang, creative energy, emotional passion, new enterprises, projective energy, religious conversion, spiritual awakening, and new financial projects. It is also an auspicious time for workings to be bold, to overcome obstacles, to take risks, to speak your mind, and to take the initiative.

In the body, this is an appropriate time for workings that are related to childbirth, epilepsy, headaches, libido, lust, migraines, pimples, polyps, ringworm, sex, smallpox, strokes, toothaches, canker sores, cleft palates, hair loss, the brain, the face, the head, the testicles, upper teeth, weight loss, high blood pressure, and kidney disease/infection. With respect to people, it is a good time for workings that are related to Botswanans, Cambodians, Danes, Germans, Israelis, Lithuanians, Pakistanis, Palestinians, Panamanians, Poles, Syrians, Vietnamese, the English, and the French. It is also an auspicious time for workings relating to entrepreneurs, explorers, idealists, optimists, and warriors. In the home, it is a great time for workings that are related to attics, ceilings, fireplaces, hardware, plaster, roofs, wallpaper, childhood possessions, and other wall coverings.

Geographically, Aries is an auspicious time for workings that are related to Botswana, Cambodia, Denmark, England, France, Germany, Israel, Lithuania, Pakistan, Palestine, Panama, Poland, Syria, and Vietnam. It is also auspicious for workings relating to barns, hills, meadows, pastures, stables, criminal lairs, sandy grounds, and places that have recently been plowed, purchased, or renovated, as well as for workings that are related to these cities: Kraków, Florence, Marseille, Naples, Nashville, and San Francisco.

Aries Correspondences
Mars/Cardinal Fire/East/Day/Tuesday/Spring

Color: pink, red, scarlet, white, yellow; with red as the prime color

Charm: musk

Animal: badger, cardinal, eagle, red-tailed hawk, magpie, porcupine, ram, robin, shark, wolf

Number: 1, 7, 9

Metal: bronze, pink gold, iron, steel

Stone: amethyst, bloodstone, carnelian, coral, diamond, garnet, red jasper, fire opal, quartz crystal, ruby, sard, sardonyx, red tourmaline

Plant: alder, allspice, angelica, asparagus, basil, beet, betony, bramble, cactus, carnation, cayenne, cedar, chestnut, cinnamon, clove, coffee, cowslip, cumin, daffodil, dandelion, deerstongue, eye of Satan ☠, fennel, fir, galangal, garlic, ginger, gorse, hemp, holly, holy thistle, honeysuckle, juniper, marjoram, mustard, onion, pepper, peppermint, pine, poppy, radish, wild rose, rosemary, sage, thistle, thorn, wild thyme, tulip, willow, woodbine, all prickly, spiny, and thorny plants and trees

Incense: cinnamon, copal, dragon's blood, frankincense, ginger, musk, myrrh

Goddess: Anath, Athena, Badb, Belat, Cybele, Durga, Hecate, Hestia, Ishtar, Macha, Medb, Minerva, the Morrigan, Neith, Nemain, Oya, Pallas Athene, Sekhmet, Tiamat, Vara

God: Ammon, Amon-Ra, Ares, Bel, Bel Marduk, Indra, Khnum, Marduk, Mars, Nergal, Pallas, Surya

Evocation: Gilgamesh, Machidiel, Samael

 ## Taurus

April 20 to May 20 or 21

This is a powerful time for voice magick, Earth magick/rituals/spells, and workings that are related to abundance, acquisition, aesthetics, affection, beauty, building, collections, comfort, crafts, creativity, determination, elegance, endurance, femininity, foundations, gardening, gentleness, handiwork, honesty, industry, integration, jealousy, love, luxury, money, orderliness, organization, ownership, passion, passivity, patience, peace, permanence, perseverance, possessions, possessiveness, practicality, privacy, prosperity, purposefulness, realism, reliability, responsibility, rigidity, sculpture, security, sensuality, serenity, stability, steadfastness, strength, tenacity, thoughtfulness, tradition, violence, wealth, workaholism, yin, cautious reactions, concrete results, creative ability, earthy love, inner peace, passionate love, real estate, receptive energy, sensual love, the home, and the material. Taurus is also an auspicious time for workings to attract abundance, acquire possessions, move house, remain steadfast, save money, strengthen purpose, buy a home, and to not give in.

In the body, this is an appropriate time for workings that are related to lust, sex, lower teeth, physical passion, physical pleasure, tactile sensation, the ears, the neck, the senses, the throat, the thyroid, venereal diseases, chronic diseases/disorders, and throat diseases/disorders/infections. In the home, this is a great time for workings that are related to basements, carpets, foundations, gardens, rugs, statues, and lower floors. With respect to people, this is a good time for workings that are related to Australians, Ecuadorians, Greeks, Iranians, Japanese, Poles, Russians, Tanzanians, the Dutch, the Irish, and the Swiss. It is also an auspicious time for workings relating to architects, artists, builders, farmers, gardeners, homebodies, industrialists, realtors, salespeople, sculptors, singers, and workaholics.

Geographically, Taurus is a powerful time for workings that are related to Australia, Ecuador, Iran, Ireland, Greece, Japan, Poland, Russia, Switzerland, and Tanzania, as well as pastures, plains, horse barns, one-story buildings, vacant land with small trees, anywhere that cattle feed or live, and land that has been recently cleared and planted with grain. It is also auspicious for workings that are related to these cities: Dublin, El Paso, Honolulu, Lucerne, and St. Louis.

Taurus Correspondences
Venus/Fixed Earth/South/Night/Friday/Midnight/Spring

Color: blue, cream, green, spring green, pink, red, turquoise, yellow, pastels; with green as the prime color

Animal: bear, beaver, bull, cow, magpie, ox, robin, white tiger, woodpecker

Number: 6

Metal: brass, bronze, copper, gold, silver

Stone: moss agate, azurite, carnelian, chrysoprase, coral, red coral, diamond, emerald, jacinth, jade, lapis lazuli, malachite, opal, peridot, pyrite, rutilated quartz, rhodonite, sapphire, topaz, golden topaz, green tourmaline, turquoise

Plant: almond, apple, apricot, artichoke, ash, asparagus, birch, bramble, cardamom, cedar, cherry, coltsfoot, cumin, cypress, daisy, dandelion, figwort, foxglove, geranium, hawthorn, heather, hibiscus, honeysuckle, hyacinth, lilac, lily, lily of the valley, lovage, magnolia, marsh mallow, mint, mugwort, myrtle, oakmoss, orchid, patchouli, pear, pepperwort, plum, plumeria, poppy, raspberry, rose, wild rose, sage, thyme, tonka bean, vanilla, vervain, violet, willow, ylang-ylang

Incense: benzoin, civet, musk, patchouli, rose, sage, storax, vanilla, violet

Goddess: Acca Larentia, Aditi, Aphrodite, Asherah, Astarte, Bast, Brigid, Fatima, Flora, Frigg, Gaia, Gefion, Hathor, Ishtar, Isis, Lakshmi, Maeve, Maia, Medb, Ninsûna, Oshun, Skadi, Tanith, Al Uzza, Vacca, Venus, Yaoji

God: Baal, Bacchus, Bran, Cernunnos, Dionysus, Horus, Indra, Jupiter, Krishna, Marduk, Min, Mithras, Osiris, Perun, Poseidon, Ptah, Serapis, Zeus

Evocation: Anael, Apis bull, Araziel, Guinevere, Hagiel, the Hyades, Io, Maid Marian, Minotaur, the Pleiades, Robin Hood

☿ Gemini

May 21 or 22 to June 20, 21, or 22

This is a powerful time for uncrossing, Air magick/rituals/spells, and workings that are related to activity, adaptability, balance, changeability, change(s), cleverness, communication, curiosity, details, diversity, duality, emotions, entertaining, gatherings, ideas, instability, intelligence, literature, money, nervousness, relationships, self-expression, sociability, speed, thoughtfulness, travel, variety, versatility, wittiness, writing, fast talking, manual dexterity, mental response, mental work, new experiences, pleasure trips, public relations, quick thinking, quick wit, and trickster energy. It is also an auspicious time for workings to be articulate, break habits, gather information, join clubs, make changes, move house, send mail, enroll in classes, open your mind, overcome mental blocks, and live in the moment.

In the body, this is a good time for workings that are related to asthma, healing, infertility, feverish ravings, nervous disorders, the arms, the chest, the hands, the lungs, the nerves, blood diseases/disorders, the shoulders, and diseases, disorders or injuries to the arms, hands, and shoulders. With respect to people, Gemini is a powerful time for workings that are related to Armenians, Belgians, Icelanders, Moroccans, Tunisians, North Americans, the Welsh, and people from northern Egypt, as well as communicators, journalists, twins, wordsmiths, writers, media personalities, and PR specialists. In the home, it is an auspicious time for workings that are related to bookshelves, chests, coffers, plaster, wainscoting, and walls.

Geographically, it is a great time for workings that are related to Armenia, Belgium, Iceland, Morocco, Tunisia, Wales, North America, northern Egypt, and the part of the United States that is east of the Mississippi, as well as barns, granaries, hills, mountains, theaters, concert halls, and high places, It is also auspicious for workings that are related to these cities: Houston, London, Melbourne, New York, San Francisco, Tacoma, and Tripoli.

Gemini Correspondences

Mercury/Mutable Air/West/Day/Wednesday/Summer

Color: black, blue, light gray, green, orange, pink, red, silver, turquoise, violet, white, saffron yellow, iridescent shades, multi-colors; with yellow and orange as the prime colors

Charm: twins, pair of obelisks

Animal: butterfly, coyote, deer, dragonfly, eagle, finch, fox, parrot, peccary, phoenix

Number: 2, 3, 5, 6, 12

Metal: chrome, gold, mercury ☠, silver

Stone: agate, moss agate, alexandrite, apophyllite, aquamarine, beryl, carbuncle, chrysocolla, chrysoprase, diamond, emerald, jade, moonstone, pearl, quartz crystal, tiger's-eye, topaz, tourmaline, bicolored and variegated stones

Plant: almond, anise, beech, bergamot, buckwheat, caraway, carrot, citron, clover, daisy, dill, elder, eyebright, fennel, fern, filbert, forget-me-not, hawthorn, hazel, High John, horehound, iris, lavender, lemongrass, lily, lily of the valley, mace, mandrake, marjoram, mugwort, nut trees, oak, parsley, pear, peas, black pepper, peppermint, rock rose, rowan, sea holly, snapdragon, lemon verbena, vervain, wormwood, yam, yarrow

Incense: dragon's blood, labdanum, mastic, mint

Goddess: Artemis, Inanna, Jaya-Vijaya, Lofn, Persephone, Sheela-na-gig, Tefnut

God: Apollo, Damuzi, Enki, Hermes, Janus, Kokopelli, Krishna, Legba, Maximon, Mercury, Odin, Shu, Thoth

Evocation: Ambriel, the Dioscuri, Odysseus, Raphael, Romulus and Remus

Cancer

June 22 to July 22 or 23

This is a powerful time for divination magick, lunar magick, psychic work, Water magick/rituals/spells, and workings that are related to balance, emotions, enterprise, generation, growth, hospitality, informality, insecurity, instincts, intuition, manipulation, mood, moodiness, nesting, nostalgia, nurture, pacifism, perception, protectiveness, secrecy, secrets, security, sensitivity, silence, vulnerability, yin, domestic matters, domestic sensitivity, emotional expression, emotional support, family life, instinctual knowledge, investment property, maternal love, paternal love, positive attitude, psychic energy, psychic sensitivity, receptive energy, the family, and the home. It is also an auspicious time to display emotions, honor deities, sharpen intuition, plead "not guilty," work on marriages, and differentiate between what you need and what you want.

In the body, this is a good time for workings that are related to cancer, edema, fertility, breast cancer, chest congestion, childhood illnesses, digestive problems, pulmonary disorders, severe coughs, the arms, the breasts, the chest, the lungs, the stomach, and stomach complaints/disorders. It is also an appropriate time for workings to gain weight. With respect to people, Cancer is an auspicious time for workings that are related to Africans, Americans, Bahamians, Canadians, Filipinos, Georgians, Iraqis, Mozambicans, Paraguayans, Scots, Somalis, Thais, New Zealanders, and the Dutch, as well as babies, children, families, homebodies, mothers, pacifists, gourmet cooks, and peace activists. In the home, it is a good time for workings that are related to antiques, basements, cisterns, fountains, heirlooms, kitchens, vases, wells, laundry rooms, and security systems.

Geographically, this is a great time for workings that are relate to Africa, Canada, Georgia, Iraq, Mozambique, Paraguay, Scotland, Somalia, Thailand, New Zealand, the Bahamas, the Netherlands, the Philippines, and the United States, as well as beaches, brooks, marshes, oceans, reservoirs, rivers, springs, riverbanks, wet ditches and trenches, and places where rushes, sedges, or sea grasses grow. It is also auspicious for workings that are related to these cities: Algiers, Amsterdam, Istanbul, Milan, New York, Santa Fe, Stockholm, Tokyo, Tunis, and Venice.

Cancer Correspondences

Moon/Cardinal Water/North/Night/Monday/Summer

Color: blue, pale blue, sky-blue, brown, smoke-gray, green, sea-green, dark green, pink, silver, ultramarine, white, pearlescent shades; with sea colors as primary

Charm: ambergris, driftwood, scarab, sea glass, seashell, shark tooth

Animal: scarab beetle, crab, duck, ibis, owl, white peacock, seagull, turtle, all crustaceans

Number: 2, 4, 5, 7

Metal: silver

Stone: agate, amber, carnelian, chalcedony, emerald, jacinth, jasper, moonstone, onyx, opal, pearl, quartz crystal, rose quartz, ruby, sapphire, sea salt, tektite, tiger's-eye, topaz, green turquoise

Plant: acanthus, adder's tongue, agrimony, alder, aloe, apple, balm, cabbage, calamus, catnip, chamomile, comfrey, daisy, eucalyptus, gardenia, geranium, ginger, holly, honeysuckle, hyssop, iris, jasmine, kiwi, lemon, lemon balm, lettuce, lily, loosestrife, lotus, marigold, marsh woundwort, mimosa, moonwort, nettle, oak, pansy, pear, pineapple, poppy, pumpkin, rose hips, white rose, wild rose, sea grass, seaweed, spruce, sundew, tomato, tuberose, lemon verbena, violet, watercress, water lily, watermelon, willow

Incense: ambergris, camphor, jasmine, myrrh, rose, sandalwood, violet

Goddess: Artemis, Ceres, Demeter, Diana, Freya, Fulla, Hera, Isis, Juno Luna, Kwan Yin, the Mother

God: Anubis, Heimdall, Kephera, Mercury, Nzambi, Toko'yoto

Evocation: Cael, Charon, Gabriel, Muriel

 # Leo

July 23 to August 22 or 23

This is a powerful time for cat magick, Fire magick/rituals/spells, and workings that are related to accidents, activity, advice, authority, birth, career, charisma, command, confidence, courage, courtesy, creativity, determination, drama, dynamism, ego, enmity, entertaining, fame, fertility, flirtation, force, friendship, gossip, growth, guidance, hobbies, honor, impressiveness, increase, jealousy, jewelry, leadership, loyalty, opulence, passion, power, pride, progress, prosperity, quarrels, recognition, self-respect, self-promotion, showmanship, sophistication, spontaneity, stability, strength, valiance, vitality, warmth, will, willpower, yang, creative energy, inner child, pleasure trips, projective energy, solar power, strong emotions, and power over others. It is also an auspicious time for workings to break habits, borrow money, inspire others, lose weight, move house, promote yourself, share information, buy a home, take the lead, and work with others.

In the body, this is a good time for workings that are related to childbirth, convulsions, infertility, jaundice, libido, plagues, pleurisy, sex, back pain, eye pain, good eyesight, heart problems, high fevers, infectious diseases, the back, the heart, the liver, the spine, the stomach, and diseases/problems in the ribs or sides. With respect to people, it is a powerful time for workings that are related to Africans, Congolese, Cypriots, Greeks, Jamaicans, Indonesians, Ivorians, Lebanese, Italians, Macedonians, Madagascans, Romanians, Singaporeans, Syrians, Zanzibarians, the Dutch, the French, and the Swiss, as well as actors, children, commanders, friends, leaders, and performers, In the home, Leo is an appropriate time for workings that are related to barbecues, chimneys, fireplaces, hearths, playrooms, fire pits, great rooms, and anything that is grand or palatial.

Geographically, it is a great time for workings that are related to Africa, Cyprus, France, Greece, Indonesia, Italy, Jamaica, Lebanon, Macedonia, Madagascar, Romania, Singapore, Switzerland, Syria, Zanzibar, the Alps, the Congo, the Netherlands, and the Ivory Coast, as well as castles, deserts, forests, forts, palaces, parks, woods, inaccessible places, rocky places, steep places, and wherever wild animals gather. It is also auspicious for workings that are related to these cities: Chicago, Damascus, Los Angeles, Madrid, Mumbai, New York, Philadelphia, Prague, and Rome.

Leo Correspondences

Sun/Fixed Fire/East/Day/Sunday/Summer

Color: green, gold, orange, red, blood red, yellow

Charm: musk

Animal: eagle, elk, griffin, lion, peacock, robin, rooster, sphinx, sturgeon, wolf

Number: 1, 4, 8, 11

Metal: gold, iron

Stone: amber, beryl, chrysolite, diamond, garnet, jacinth, jasper, morganite, onyx, peridot, ruby, rose quartz, sapphire, sardonyx, tiger's-eye, topaz, tourmaline

Plant: acacia, almond, angelica, anise, balm, banana, benzoin, borage, clove carnation, celandine, chicory, cinnamon, cinquefoil, citron, clove, columbine, copal, coriander, corn, cyclamen, dandelion, dill, eyebright, goldenseal, grapefruit, hawthorn, hazel, heliotrope, holly, hops, juniper, laurel, lemon, lime, marigold, marjoram, mint, motherwort, nutmeg, oak, orange, palm, passionflower, peony, potentilla, raspberry, rhododendron, rosemary, rue, saffron, sage, silverweed, St. John's wort, sunflower, tormentil, vine, willow, all citrus fruits and trees

Incense: amber, copal, frankincense, mint, musk, myrrh, olibanum, rosemary, saffron, sandalwood, wood aloes

Goddess: Anath, Asherah, Atalanta, Athirat, Bast, Cybele, Devi, Diana, Durga, Freya, Frigg, Hathor, Hera, Hlyn, Inanna, Ishtar, Juno, Nana, Qadesh, Rhea, Sekhmet, Sesheta, Tefnut, Al Uzza

God: Aker, Amon, Aton, Atum, Helios, Horus, Ishkur, Khenti-Amenti, Mithras, Nergal, Ra (Great Cat of Heliopolis), Vishnu

Evocation: Hercules, Michael, Omphale, Seratiel, Verchiel

Virgo

August 23 to September 22

This is a powerful time for astrology, numerology, Earth magick/rituals/spells, and workings that are related to accomplishment, adaptability, analysis, assimilation, cleanliness, computers, concentration, crafts, criticism, details, discretion, education, employment, facts, fate, favors, frugality, handiwork, incisiveness, independence, information, jobs, judiciousness, logic, melancholy, objectivity, operation, order, organization, passivity, perfection, practicality, progress, prudence, purification, reason, research, resourcefulness, scheduling, science, self-criticism, sensibility, service, stability, tranquility, selectivity, understanding, wit, work, analytical thinking, business success, emotional detachment, goodwill, intellectual detachment, intellectual matters, mental adjustment(s), platonic love, precise thought, receptive energy, and the mind. It is also an auspicious time for workings to command, perfect, appreciate yourself, break habits, complete tasks, control sexuality, find truth, provide services, send mail, enroll in classes, obey fate without struggle, and transform negative emotions into compassion.

In the body, it is a good time for workings that are related to diet, gas, healing, health, indigestion, infertility, bowel problems, psychosomatic illness, the abdomen, the bowels, the intestines, the nerves, stomach diseases/disorders, testicular diseases/disorders, the brow chakra, and the sympathetic nervous system. With respect to people, Virgo is a great time for workings that are related to Brazilians, Congolese, Croatians, Cubans, Dominicans, Greeks, Haitians, Iraqis, Jamaicans, Kurds, Turks, Uruguayans, Venezuelans, Vietnamese, Puerto Ricans, the Swiss, and all those who are from the Caribbean, as well as accountants, nurses, workers, dental hygienists, domestic staff, and financial planners. In the home, it is an auspicious time for workings that are related to closets, crafts, desks, gardens, studios, dining rooms, fitness equipment, and wicker furniture.

Geographically, this is a powerful time for workings that are related to Brazil, Croatia, Greece, Iraq, Switzerland, Turkey, Uruguay, Venezuela, the Congo, Vietnam, and the West Indies, as well as dairies, granaries, libraries, spas, grain fields, and health resorts. It is also auspicious for workings that are related to these cities: Athens, Baghdad, Boston, Jerusalem, Liverpool, Los Angeles, and Paris.

Virgo Correspondences

Mercury/Mutable Earth/South/Night/Wednesday/Summer

Color: black, pale blue, navy blue, brown, gold, gray, green, orange, peach, pink, purple, tan, violet, white, yellow, pastels, patterns, marbled colors

Charm: caduceus, scales, sword, virgin

Animal: brown bear, bee, dove, mouse, rooster, squirrel, unicorn

Number: 5, 6, 9, 10, 11

Metal: gold, mercury ☠, nickel, platinum

Stone: agate, moss agate, amethyst, apatite, aquamarine, aventurine, azurite, carnelian, celestite, chrysolite, diamond, emerald, fluorite, jacinth, green jade, jasper, pink jasper, lapis lazuli, marble, opal, peridot, rhodochrosite, sapphire, star sapphire, sardonyx, smithsonite, topaz, blue topaz, turquoise, zircon

Plant: almond, ash, aster, bergamot, birch, broom, calamint, caraway, cedar, cherry, chrysanthemum, corn, cornflower, cotoneaster, cypress, dill, edelweiss, elder, eyebright, fennel, fern, gorse, hazel, honeysuckle, horehound, hyacinth, ivy, lavender, lily, lily of the valley, mace, madonna lily, marjoram, millet, moss, narcissus, nuts, oats, pansy, parsley, peppermint, potato, rice, rosemary, rye, savory, scullcap, turnip, valerian, vervain, violet, alpine flowers, root vegetables, and flowering plants that grow on rocks

Incense: lavender, mint, patchouli, rosemary, sandalwood, violet

Goddess: Aditi, Anath, Arianrhod, Artemis, Ashtoreth, Astraea, Atalanta, Atargatis, Athena, Ceres, Cybele, Damkina, Demeter, Diana, Dike, Erigone, Fatima, Frimla, Hera, Hestia, Ho Hsien-Ku, Ilmatar, Inanna, Iris, Ishtar, Isis, Kore, Luonnotar, Mary (Virgo Maria), Minerva, Nana, Narisah, Neith, Pallas Athene, Parthenos, Persephone, Prosperine, Spenta Armaiti, Tyche, Al Uzza, Vesta, Xochiquetzal, the Zorya

God: Forseti, Ogma

Evocation: Daphne, Delilah, Hamaliel, Raphael, Syn, Voel

Libra

September 23 to October 22 or 23

This is a powerful time for Air magick/rituals/spells and workings that are related to activity, artistry, attraction, balance, beauty, calm, caution, choice, civility, clubs, composure, compromise, cooperation, diplomacy, enterprise, entertaining, equilibrium, fairness, fashion, favors, femininity, gentleness, grace, harmony, indecision, interaction, justice, longevity, love, manipulation, manners, marriage, negotiation, partnership, peace, perceptiveness, procrastination, quiet, reaction, refinement, romance, seduction, self-awareness, self-examination, self-image, sensitivity, sensuality, sexuality, talent, thoughtfulness, union(s), yang, artistic work, emotional balance, idealistic love, investment property, joint action, karmic balance, law enforcement, legal matters, mental stimulation, mental work, romantic love, social graces, spiritual balance, and peace and quiet. It is also an auspicious time for workings to listen, be diplomatic, create beauty, make compromises, restore harmony, and balance positive and negative forces.

In the body, it is a good time for workings that are related to back problems, blood poisoning, groin problems, the buttocks, the groin, the kidneys, the thighs, kidney diseases/infections, kidney/urinary stones, and the lower back. With respect to people, Libra is an appropriate time for workings that are related to Argentineans, Austrians, Belgians, Botswanans, Burmese, Canadians, Chinese, Fijians, Japanese, Nigerians, Siberians, Tibetans, Ugandans, Uzbeks, and people from northern India or southern Egypt, as well as arbitrators, artists, cosmeticians, couples, designers, diplomats, judges, lawyers, marriage counselors, negotiators, partners, and statespeople. In the home, it is an auspicious time for workings that are related to attics, outbuildings, roofs, rooms-within-rooms, wardrobes, clothes closets, furniture tops, tree houses, and upper floors.

Geographically, it is a great time for workings that are related to Argentina, Austria, Belgium, Botswana, Canada, China, Fiji, Japan, Myanmar, Nigeria, Siberia, Tibet, Uganda, Uzbekistan, northern India, and southern Egypt, as well as hillsides, mountaintops, sawmills, skyscrapers, treetops, windmills, hunting grounds, sandy places, and any place that is frequented by hawks or has very clean air. It is also auspicious for workings that are related to these cities: Antwerp, Copenhagen, Frankfurt, Johannesburg, Knoxville, Leeds, Lisbon, and Vienna.

Libra Correspondences

Venus/Cardinal Air/West/Day/Friday/Autumn

Color: black, blue, cerulean blue, royal blue, brown, light green, pink, rose, yellow, pastels

Charm: claws, scales, sugar, sword, maple syrup

Animal: deer, dove, hare, rabbit, raven, sparrow, swan

Number: 6, 7, 8, 11

Metal: aluminum, bronze, copper, all metals

Stone: agate, fire agate, aquamarine, beryl, carnelian, celestite, coral, chrysolite, diamond, emerald, jacinth, jade, jasper, lapis lazuli, malachite, opal, rose quartz, sapphire, sard, tourmaline

Plant: almond, apple, apple blossom, bamboo, banana, bean, catnip, clematis, cyclamen, daisy, foxglove, *Justicia*, kidneywort, lemon, lilac, lily, lotus, magnolia, mango, maple, marjoram, mint, mugwort, mullein, myrtle, narcissus, orchid, passionflower, pennyroyal, persimmon, plum, plumeria, pumpkin, rose, white rose, shower of gold, spearmint, squash, sugar cane, sweet pea, sweet potato, thyme, tomato, vanilla, lemon verbena, vervain, violet, vine, walnut, yam

Incense: galbanum, mint, rose, vanilla, violet

Goddess: Astraea, Athena, Dike, Isis, Justitia, Ma'at, Minerva, Nemesis, Psyche, Saga, Themis, Tyche, Unk, Venus, Yemaya

God: Cernunnos, Hephaestus, the Horned God, Inyan, Mithras, Nagi, Njoerd, Orunmila, Shango, Shiva, Thoth, Tyr, Vishnu, Vulcan

Evocation: Anael, Hadakiel, Hagiel, Uriel, Zuriel

 ## Scorpio

October 23 to November 21 or 23

This is a powerful time for clairvoyance, divination, night magick, sex magick, Water magick/rituals/spells, and workings that are related to accidents, anger, changes, control, creativity, death, deceit, desire, destruction, detection, emotions, growth, intensity, investigation, jealousy, leadership, loyalty, manipulation, mysteries, mysticism, observation, obsession, passion, perception, perversion, power, purification, puzzles, rebirth, recycling, regeneration, renewal, revenge, secrecy, secretiveness, secrets, self-awareness, self-destruction, sexuality, shrewdness, spirituality, stability, subtlety, success, transformation, transmutation, willpower, wisdom, emotional depths, emotional expression, emotional rebirth, healing power, inner depths, inner power, magickal power(s), occult initiation, psychic awareness, psychic energy, psychic growth, psychic power(s), receptive energy, sexual energy, sexual love, sexual matters, sexual power, spiritual investigation, the afterlife, the occult, the Underworld, the unknown, the deep unconscious, the healing touch, and use of power. It is also an auspicious time for workings to end connections, move house, save money, uncover secrets, use power, and buy a home.

In the body, it is a good time for workings that are related to fertility, healing, hemorrhoids, lust, priapism, sex, bladder stones, groin injuries, sperm disorders, urinary gravel, the genitals, the prostate, the testicles, the womb, male reproductive organs, genital diseases/disorders, prostate diseases/disorders, the lower abdomen, and the sex glands. This is also a good time to channel healing energy, and for workings to gain weight. With respect to people, it is a powerful time for workings that are related to Algerians, Angolans, Brazilians, Dominicans, Hondurans, Koreans, Moroccans, Norwegians, Palestinians, Panamanians, Paraguayans, Poles, Syrians, Turks, Zambians, Zimbabweans, and South Africans, as well as dentists, detectives, hypnotists, investigators, mystics, psychiatrists, researchers, and sorcerers. In the home, Scorpio is a great time for workings that are related to antiques, artifacts, bathrooms, gardens, kitchens, ottomans, pantries, renovations, sinks, crawl spaces, exotic items, floor cushions, and laundry rooms.

Geographically, it is an appropriate time for workings that are related to Algeria, Angola, Honduras, Korea, Morocco, Norway, Palestine, Panama, Paraguay, Poland, Syria, Turkey, Zambia, Zimbabwe, South Africa, and the Dominican Republic, as well as moors, orchards, ponds, quagmires, ruins, sinkholes, vineyards, muddy places, stagnant lakes, abandoned homes near water, and wherever creeping and crawling creatures can be found. It is also auspicious for workings that are related to these cities: Baltimore, Cincinnati, Frankfurt, Ghent, Halifax, Little Rock, Liverpool, New Haven, New Orleans, Philadelphia, Providence, Washington DC, and West Palm Beach.

Scorpio Correspondences

Pluto/Mars/Fixed Water/North/Night/Tuesday/Autumn

Color: black, brown, gray, maroon, orange, red, dark red

Charm: ambergris, uraeus

Animal: butterfly, cobra, dog, eagle, hawk, lizard, lobster, owl, panther, phoenix, scorpion, snake, vulture, wolf

Number: 0, 8, 9

Metal: copper, gold, iron, plutonium ☠, silver, steel

Stone: agate, amethyst, aquamarine, beryl, bloodstone, carbuncle, charoite, citrine, coral, garnet, geode, hawk's eye, jasper, jet, lodestone, malachite, obsidian, opal, pearl, rutilated quartz, ruby, salt, sardonyx, topaz, turquoise, zircon

Plant: acacia, allspice, ash, azalea, basil, blackthorn, cedar, chili pepper, chrysanthemum, clove, cumin, dahlia, deerstongue, dill, eggplant, galangal, gardenia, garlic, geranium, ginger, gladiola, heather, hellebore, holly, honeysuckle, hops, horehound, ivy, lemon balm, nettle, orchid, pine, pomegranate, reed, rhododendron, rhubarb, saffron, sarsaparilla, scorpion-grass, scorpion weed, thistle, vanilla, vetiver, violet, yew, all carnivorous plants

Fungus: all mushrooms

Incense: ambergris, benzoin, cedar, myrrh, opoponax, patchouli, vanilla, violet

Goddess: Adsagsona, Cerridwen, Eir, Ereshkigal, Hecate, Hel, Ishhara, Isis, Lilith, the Morrigan, Persephone, Prosperine, Prosymna, Sedna, Selqet, Tiamat

God: Anubis, Hades, Mars, Maximon, Njoerd, Osiris, Pluto, Set

Evocation: Ahriman, Azrael, Barbiel, Richol

❧ Sagittarius

November 22/23 to December 21/22

This is a powerful time for clairvoyance, horse magick, Fire magick/rituals/spells, and workings that are related to activity, adaptability, administration, adventure, ambition, aspiration, charisma, confidence, courage, danger, education, energy, expansion, experimentation, exploration, fearlessness, force, forgiveness, freedom, friendliness, government, honesty, hunting, imagination, joviality, laws, learning, movement, optimism, passion, philosophy, progressiveness, prophecy, publications, rebellion, religion, self-confidence, self-sacrifice, sexuality, sports, studies, tolerance, travel, truth, truthfulness, wisdom, writing, business travel, court cases, creative energy, honest communication, legal matters, metaphysical laws, optimistic reactions, personal space, positive change, projective energy, religious life, spiritual evolution, strategic plans, the future, the unconventional, and horseback-riding accidents. This is also an auspicious time for workings to aim higher, correct things, look ahead, send mail, expand a business, get a loan, and see the truth.

In the body, it is a good time for workings that are related to addiction, fevers, physical strength, sports injuries, the buttocks, the groin, the hips, the liver, the thighs, weight loss, and diseases that are caused by insects or unsanitary conditions. With respect to people, this is a powerful time for workings that are related to Australians, Barbadians, Chileans, Colombians, Czechs, Finns, Hispanics, Hungarians, Kenyans, Saudis, Singaporeans, Swedes, South Africans, and the Irish, as well as administrators, adventurers, archers, educators, explorers, hunters, optimists, philosophers, professors, rebels, travelers, and writers. In the home, Sagittarius is an auspicious time for workings that are related to books, fur rugs, metal cookware, religious items, upstairs rooms, wood furniture, and the areas near fireplaces.

Geographically, it is a great time for workings that are related to Australia, Barbados, Chile, Colombia, the Czech Republic, Finland, Hungary,

Ireland, Kenya, Singapore, Slovakia, Spain, Sweden, Saudi Arabia, and South Africa, as well as countrysides, elevations, fields, hills, highlands, horse barns, large estates, open spaces, and any place associated with horses. It is also auspicious for workings that are related to these cities: Budapest, Cologne, Memphis, Naples, San Diego, Spokane, Stuttgart, Tampa, and Toronto.

Sagittarius Correspondences
Jupiter/Mutable Fire/East/Day/Thursday/Autumn

Color: black, bright blue, dark blue, gold, indigo, mauve, purple (all shades), red, silver, yellow, patterns

Charm: archer, arrow, bow, centaur, quiver of arrows

Animal: dog, eagle, elephant, elk, Canadian goose, horse, lion, mare, peacock

Number: 3, 4

Metal: brass, copper, gold, pewter, tin

Stone: amethyst, carbuncle, chrysolite, emerald, jacinth, lapis lazuli, malachite, obsidian, opal, sapphire, yellow sapphire, sodalite, sugilite, topaz, turquoise, zircon

Plant: anise, basil, blueberry, burdock, carnation, cedar, chamomile, chervil, chestnut, chicory, clove, red clover, cranberry, dahlia, daisy, deerstongue, eggplant, elder, fig, ginger, grapevine, holly, honeysuckle, hydrangea, hyssop, iris, juniper, lime, marigold, mugwort, mulberry, myrtle, nutmeg, oak, oakmoss, orange, parsley, peony, pimpernel, reed, rose, rosemary, sage, St. John's wort, sassafras, black spruce, star anise, vervain, wallflower, dried fruit

Incense: copal, dragon's blood, frankincense, ginger, rose, rosemary, sage, wood aloes

Goddess: Anath, Artemis, Atalanta, Athena, Athene Hippia, Diana, Epona, Isis, Rhiannon, Rigantona, Satis, Vesta

God: Apollo, Cronos, Hades, Jupiter, Mars, Nergal

Evocation: Adnachiel, Amazons, Antiope, Cassandra, centaurs, Chiron, Crotus, Gna, Leucippe, Okyale, Pandarus, Pegasus, Sachiel, Sleipnir, Teucer

⚜ Capricorn

December 22 to January 19, 20, or 21

This is a powerful time for telepathy, Earth magick/rituals/spells, and workings that are related to achievement, ambition, business, career, caution, cold, commitment, confidence, conservatism, crafts, control, death, details, direction, discipline, efficiency, enterprise, favor, goals, handiwork, harvest, industriousness, longevity, love, manifestation, materialism, maturity, methodology, negativity, opportunism, organization, passivity, perseverance, politics, practicality, precaution, priorities, production, professionalism, prosperity, prudence, purpose, reality, recognition, respectability, responsibility, selectivity, self-discipline, self-sufficiency, stability, structure, study, success, tenacity, tradition, utilization, wisdom, wit, yang, basic needs, calculated actions, creature comforts, financial security, hard work, investment property, organizational ability, planned action, psychic messages, receptive energy, social climbing, social respectability, and upward movement. It is also an auspicious time to be careful, get organized, increase status, make plans, save money, overcome obstacles, push yourself, and send messages over long distances.

In the body, this is a good time for workings that are related to depression, lust, rashes, joint pain, knee problems, psychosomatic illness, the bones, the hair, the joints, the knees, the skin, the teeth, and skin diseases/disorders. With respect to people, it is an appropriate time for workings that are related to Afghanis, Albanians, Australians, Bosnians, Bulgarians, Burmese, Cameroonians, Cubans, Greeks, Haitians, Indians, Iranians, Lebanese, Lithuanians, Mexicans, Sudanese, and the British, as well as architects, bosses, conservatives, fathers, opportunists, politicians, scientists, socialites, corporate leaders, and prominent persons. In the home, Capricorn is an auspicious time for workings that are related to antiques, chandeliers, pottery, sculptures, stonework, woodsheds, dark places, exposed bricks, fine art, leather furniture, the threshold, and wood furniture.

Geographically, it is a great time for workings that are related to Afghanistan, Albania, Australia, Bosnia, Bulgaria, Cameroon, Cuba, Greece, Haiti, India, Iran, Lebanon, Lithuania, Mexico, Myanmar, Sudan, and the United Kingdom, as well as barns, barren fields, bushy places, compost piles, fallow ground, single-story buildings, thorny places, and anywhere that is associated with sheep, sail-making, or animal husbandry. It is also auspicious for workings that are related to these cities: Atlanta, Brussels, Ghent, Mexico City, New Delhi, New York, Salt Lake City, and Seattle.

Capricorn Correspondences
Saturn/Cardinal Earth/South/Night/Saturday/Winter

Color: black, blue, royal blue, brown, dark brown, dark gray, dark green, indigo, red, russet, violet, white

Charm: civet, conch shell, goat horn, musk

Animal: beaver, dog, elephant, falcon, goat, mountain goat, sea goat, ibex, snow goose, owl, woodpecker

Number: 3, 8

Metal: electrum, gold, lead ☠, pewter, silver

Stone: black amber, amethyst, azurite, beryl, bloodstone, carnelian, chalcedony, chrysoprase, coal, diamond, black diamond, garnet, all gems, granite, jet, lapis lazuli, malachite, moonstone, obsidian, black opal, onyx, white-banded onyx, quartz crystal, rose quartz, smoky quartz, ruby, sapphire, white sapphire, sardonyx, green tourmaline, turquoise, yellow zircon

Plant: asafetida, barley, beet, birch, bonsai trees, Brussels sprout, cabbage, carnation, comfrey, cypress, daisy, dock, elder, elm, gardenia, ginger, holly, honeysuckle, horsetail, ivy, jasmine, kale, long pepper, narcissus, nightshade, magnolia, mimosa, mint, oakmoss, oregano, pansy, paprika, pine, poplar, poppy, rowan, rue, sassafras, sedum, slippery elm, snowdrop, sorrel, spinach, spruce, thyme, vervain, vetiver, violet, wisteria, woodruff, yew

Incense: benzoin, civet, jasmine, mint, musk, patchouli

Goddess: Amba, Aphrodite, Aphrodite of the Goats, Awehai, Freya, Gaia, Gula, Hecate, Juno, Juno Caprotina, Mylitta, Olwen, Vesta, Vor

God: Aegipan, Agni, Baal Gad, Dionysus, Ea, Enki, Faunus, Freyr, the Horned God, Leshy, Oannes, Pan, Perun, Priapus, Saturn, Thor

Evocation: Amalthea, Azazel, Cambiel, Capricornus, Cassiel, Gabriel, Ganymede, Hanael, Satan, satyrs

 Aquarius

January 20/21 to February 18, 19, 20

This is a powerful time for ESP, dream work, Air magick/rituals/spells, Water magick/rituals/spells, and workings that are related to activity, altruism, aspiration, charity, civility, compassion, creativity, entertaining, equality, experiments, fellowship, freedom, friendship, friendliness, gentleness, hope, humanitarianism, humor, idealism, indifference, individualism, intuition, inventiveness, knowledge, loyalty, magnanimity, objectivity, paradoxes, rebellion, science, stability, sympathy, thoughtfulness, tolerance, uniqueness, unpredictability, unselfishness, creative expression, eternal life, evolutionary growth, group understanding, higher consciousness, intellectual creativity, mental work, personal freedom, pleasure trips, psychic ability, psychic sensitivity, public service, quantum physics, quick thinking, sudden change(s), the unconventional, universal friendship, and freedom of choice. It is also an auspicious time to make libations, and for workings to borrow money, defy conventions, join clubs, move house, open minds, solve problems, buy a home, end bad habits, and get in touch with the universal healing force.

In the body, it is a good time for workings that are related to addiction(s), gas, healing, insomnia, holistic medicine, leg cramps, muscle spasms, nervous disorders, the ankles, the blood, the calves, the legs, the shins, weight loss, leg injuries/problems, the circulatory system, and to break addictions. With respect to people, it is an auspicious time for workings that are related to Afghanis, Azerbaijanis, Chileans, Ethiopians, Finns, Iranians, Israelis, Japanese, Lithuanians, Mexicans, Poles, Russians, Swedes, Syrians, Turkmen, Yugoslavians, Costa Ricans, and the English, as well as activists, anarchists, astrologers, eccentrics, humanitarians, idealists, individualists, intellectuals, inventors, philanthropists, progressives, rebels, researchers, revolutionaries, scientists, computer techs, public servants, software developers, and unique characters. In the home, Aquarius is a great time for workings that are related to appliances, blinds, carvings, eaves, roofs, shutters, contemporary decor, elevated beds, huge windows, modern art, open floor plans, and upper floors.

Geographically, it is a powerful time for workings that are related to Afghanistan, Azerbaijan, Chile, Costa Rica, England, Ethiopia, Finland, Iran, Israel, Japan, Lithuania, Mexico, Poland, Russia, Sweden, Syria, Turkmenistan, and Yugoslavia, as well as airy places, hilly areas, open spaces, rock quarries, stony land, uneven ground, land around springs, vineyards, any location from which minerals have been removed, and places that have newly been plowed or otherwise dug up. It is also auspicious for workings that are related to these cities: Dallas, Hamburg, Helsinki, Indianapolis, Milwaukee, Moscow, and Salzburg.

Aquarius Correspondences

Uranus/Saturn/Fixed Air/West/Day/Saturday/Thursday/Winter

Color: blue (all shades), electric blue, light blue, green, indigo, hot pink, silver, turquoise, ultramarine, violet, pale yellow, all colors, multi-colors, fluorescent shades; with blue as the primary color

Charm: star, water bearer, water jar

Animal: albatross, buffalo, cuckoo, dog, hummingbird, ostrich, otter, phoenix, all very large birds

Number: 2, 3, 11

Metal: aluminum, lead ☠, silver, stainless steel, titanium, uranium ☠, zinc, all metals

Element: cobalt

Stone: amber, amethyst, aquamarine, boji stone, celestite, chalcedony, white coral, garnet, jacinth, labradorite, lapis lazuli, malachite, moonstone, onyx, opal, pearl, clear quartz crystal, sapphire, zircon

Plant: acacia, allspice, almond, anise, apple, ash, aspen, azalea, bistort, bittersweet, celery, cherry, chive, citron, coriander, cypress, dandelion, dogwood, eucalyptus, euphorbia, foxglove, hibiscus, hydrangea, iris, lavender, mace, Madagascar periwinkle, mimosa, myrrh, orchid, pansy, pear, pelargonium, peppermint, pine, pitcher plant, poppy, rosemary, rowan, sage, sesame seed, snowdrop, sweet cicely, lemon verbena, violet, water violet

Incense: benzoin, frankincense, galbanum, lavender, mastic, mint, patchouli, rosemary, sage, sandalwood, violet

Goddess: Astarte, Gula, Hebe, Ishtar, Isis, Juno, Juno Februa, Nut, Sarasvatt, Sjofn

God: Ea, Hapy, Ouranos, Rimmon, Uranus, Varuna

Evocation: Cambiel, Cecrops, Deucalon, Ganymede, Uriel, Utnapishtim

Pisces

February 19 or 20 to March 20 or 21

This is a powerful time for clairvoyance, divination, ESP, releasing, telepathy, dream work, psychic work, spirit communication, past-life work, Water magick/rituals/spells, and workings that are related to adaptability, appreciation, art, belief, compassion, death, emotions, empathy, endings, eternity, hibernation, illusion, imagination, inspiration, intuition, justice, music, mystery, mysticism, passivity, poetry, privacy, reflection, reorganization, romance, sensitivity, subtlety, surrender, trust, union, vulnerability, withdrawal, yin, emotional expression, emotional responses, mystical inspiration, psychic awareness, psychic connections, psychic dreams, psychic energy, receptive energy, spiritual inspiration, the arts, and the spiritual self. It is also an auspicious time for workings to borrow money and send mail.

In the body, this is a good time for workings that are related to acne, boils, fibromyalgia, gout, lameness, rashes, slow metabolism, the feet, the toes, ulcerated sores, foot diseases/problems, low blood pressure, the lymph glands, and the lymphatic system. Pisces is also an appropriate time for workings to gain weight. In the home, it is auspicious for workings that are related to bathrooms, fountains, plumbing, ponds, and fish tanks. With respect to people, this is a great time for workings that are related to Algerians, Danes, Egyptians, Ethiopians, Ghanians, Libyans, Mongolians, Moroccans, Norwegians, Portuguese, Samoans, Sudanese, Swedes, Tunisians, and South Asians, as well as artists, believers, empaths, musicians, mystics, poets, and psychics.

Geographically, this is a powerful time for workings that relate to Algeria, Egypt, Ethiopia, Ghana, Libya, Mongolia, Morocco, Norway, Portugal, Samoa, Sudan, Sweden, Tunisia, and South Asia, as well as hermitages, moats, pumps, springs, wells, wetlands, fishponds, standing water, water mills, rivers with many fish, and places where waterfowl gather. It is also auspicious for workings that are related to these cities: Alexandria (Egypt), Jerusalem, Phoenix, San Antonio, San Francisco, Seville, and Warsaw.

Pisces Correspondences

Neptune/Jupiter/Mutable Water/North/Night/Thursday/Winter

Color: aqua, azure, blue, pale blue, green, sea green, indigo, lavender, purple, turquoise, violet, white, light yellow

Charm: ambergris, fish oil, image of two fish chained together

Animal: catfish, all fish, ox, sandpiper, seal, sheep, stork, swan, waterfowl

Number: 3, 6, 11

Metal: electrum, silver, tin, platinum, all alloys

Stone: amethyst, aquamarine, bloodstone, chrysolite, coral, diamond, emerald, jade, jasper, moonstone, mother-of-pearl, sapphire, topaz, tourmaline, turquoise

Plant: alder, aloe, anise, ash, calamus, catnip, carnation, clove, cotton, dahlia, delphinium, elm, eucalyptus, fig, gardenia, hartwort, heliotrope, honeysuckle, hyacinth, Irish moss, jasmine, laurel, lavender, lemon, lovage, mimosa, peach, Norfolk Island pine, nutmeg, opium poppy ☠, orris, rue, sage, sarsaparilla, star anise, sweet pea, water lily, willow

Incense: ambergris, jasmine, lavender, sage, sandalwood, storax

Goddess: Aphrodite the Fish, Atargatis, Atargatis Derketo, Athirat, Dea Syria, Derceto, Diana, Mari, Mary, Nehalennia, Nina, Saga, Sedna, Snotra, Urania, Venus, Yemaya

God: Cupid, Dylan, Ea, Enki, Eros, Jesus, Neptune, Poseidon, Tethra, Varuna, Vishnu

Evocation: Barchiel, Verchiel

Days of the Week

All days are ruled by the Celtic god Dis, Lord of the Seven-day Week. Each day is ruled by a different heavenly body. It has its own unique energy, its own correspondences, and is a powerful time for specific types of workings.

✺ Sunday (Sun-day)

Sunday is a powerful day for divination, psychic work, solar magick, wish magick, and workings that are related to abundance, accomplishment, achievement, action, advancement, ambition, arrogance, attraction, authority, banking, bigotry, bioenergy, business, career, charm, conception, confidence, creativity, crops, defense, drama, ego, employment, enlightenment, exorcism, expression, fame, fatherhood, favor, finances, freedom, friendship, fun, goals, growth, happiness, honor, hope, illumination, inception, individuality, innocence, joy, judgment, kindness, labor, law, leadership, learning, light, money, nobility, openness, perception, performance, power, pride, promotion(s), prosperity, protection, purchasing, purification, purity, reason, sales, self-confidence, self-knowledge, speculation, spirituality, strength, success, vitality, volunteerism, warmth, will, willpower, wisdom, career goals, civil services, creative power, divine power, financial gain, legal matters, magickal energy, male Mysteries, performing arts, personal advancement, personal finances, personal fulfillment, professional success, the self, volunteer organizations, the male principle, and the male side of women.

With respect to people, Sunday is auspicious for workings that are related to actors, bankers, bigots, brothers, children, employers, fathers, husbands, judges, leaders, men, nobles, performers, salespeople, superiors, volunteers, authority figures, businesspeople, civil servants, famous people, male partners, and world leaders. Geographically, it is a great day for workings that are related to banks, courts, fairs, and theaters. In the body, it is appropriate for workings that are related to healing, health, physical energy, physical strength, and the crown chakra.

It is also an auspicious day to begin any magickal operation, and for workings to activate change, attain goals, banish evil, end enmity, get favors, obtain honors, overcome disabilities, boost ritual energy, acquire gold or jewels, attract attention, blessings, or money. Rosewater mixed with an infusion of saffron threads can be used as a magickal ink before dawn on Sundays, especially the first Sunday of a month.

Sunday Correspondences

Sun/Fire/North/Male/Leo

Color: gold, orange, peach, red, ultraviolet, white, yellow

Number: 1, 6, 7

Metal: gold

Charm: ambergris, gold jewelry, neroli, scepter, yellow garments

Stone: agate, amber, orange calcite, carnelian, citrine, diamond, ruby, quartz crystal, pipestone, sunstone, tiger's-eye, topaz, zircon

Element: sulfur

Animal: eagle, lion, hawk, red horse, white horse, rooster, white rooster, totem animals

Plant: acacia, amaranth, anise, beech, birch, buttercup, catnip, cedar, chicory, cinnamon, clove, cowslip, galangal, heliotrope, hops, juniper, laurel, lemon, red lotus, marigold, marjoram, mistletoe, oak, orange, bitter orange, rosemary, rowan, rue, saffron, sunflower, thyme

Incense: amber, ambergris, benzoin, brimstone, cedar, cinnamon, clove, dragon's blood, frankincense, labdanum, mastic, musk, myrrh, olibanum, rosemary, sandalwood, storax, wood aloes, all gum resins

Goddess: Amaterasu (Divine Illuminator), Bast, Creiddylad, Graine, Gull-veig, Juno (Light of Heaven), Melusine, Phoebe, Saule, Sekhmet, Shapshu (Torch of the Gods), Sunna

God: Agni, An, Angus, Apollo, Baal, Balder, Bel, Cernunnos, Frey, Helios, Lugh, Mithras, Ogma, Ra (Lord of Rays), Ravikiran, Shamash, Shiva, Sol, Surya (Thousand-Rayed, Illuminator of Infinite Causes)

Evocation: Anael, Cassiel, Dardiel, Gabriel, Hercules, Hurtapel, Michael, Raphael, Sachiel, Samael

✑ Monday (Moon-day)

Monday is a powerful day for astrology, clairvoyance, divination, meditation, shape-shifting, astral projection, dream work, lucid dreaming, lunar magick, past-life work, psychic work, sea rituals/spells, Water magick/rituals/spells, and workings that are related to agriculture, antiques, archetypes, awareness, birth, calm, caring, changes, compassion, conformity, cooking, creativity, dreams, emotions, fluids, friendship, imagination, initiation, instincts, intuition, justice, longevity, love, loyalty, moods, nursing, nurture, order, peace, psychology, purity, protection, reincarnation, relocation, secrets, sincerity, spirituality, theft, travel, trust, truth, visions, domestic matters, emotional healing, female fertility, female issues, female Mysteries, lunar power, psychic ability, psychic awareness, religious experiences, short trips, spiritual growth, the home, the soul, the subconscious, the female principle, and the female side of men.

With respect to people, Monday is auspicious for workings that are related to astrologers, children, cooks, doctors, farmers, friends, mothers, nurses, psychics, psychologists, sisters, thieves, travelers, wives, women, family members, female partners, and the public. Geographically, it is a great day for workings that are related to clinics, docks, farms, hospitals, antique shops, medical offices, the sea, train stations, and all bodies of water. In the body, it is appropriate for workings that are related to fertility, healing, medicine, body fluids, the sacral chakras, and to heal wounds. It is also an auspicious day for workings to acquire silver, discover secrets, plan trips, speed horses, and avert doubt(s) or fear(s).

Monday Correspondences
Moon/Water/East/West/Female/Cancer

Color: light blue, cream, light gray, sea-green, lavender, orange, pale pink, silver, tan, pale violet, white, pearlescent colors

Number: 1, 2

Metal: silver

Charm: arrow, sea-green or silver garments, menstrual blood

Stone: aquamarine, fluorite, geode, moonstone, mother-of-pearl, pearl, clear quartz crystal, pink tourmaline

Animal: cattle, deer, frog, goose, small animals, totem animals

Plant: adder's tongue, African violet, aloe vera, basil, birch, cockscomb, coconut, eucalyptus, gardenia, honeysuckle, hyssop, white iris, jasmine, lavender, white lily, lime blossom, motherwort, myrtle, night-blooming flowers, orris root, parsley, peppermint, white poppy, rice, red rose, white rose, vervain, wallflower, willow, wormwood

Incense: ambergris, camphor, coconut, frankincense, jasmine, mastic, myrrh, rose, rosemary, sandalwood, wood aloes, and all incense made from aromatic leaves

Goddess: Arianrhod, Artemis, Athena, Bast, Blodeuwedd, Boann, Cerridwen, the Crone, Diana, the Goddess, Hera, Idunn, Inanna, Isis, Juno, Luna, Macha, Minerva, Nephthys, Nerthus, Ninhursag, Nyx, Ostara, Persephone, Rhiannon, Selene, Sif

God: Aegir, Chandra, Nanna, Ömölu, Rama, Shiva Somantha (Lord of the Moon), Sin, Soma, Surya, Thoth

Evocation: Gabriel, Merlin, Michael, Samael

❧ Tuesday (Tiu's day)

This day is named for the Norse sky and war god. The many variations of his name include Teu, Tiu, Tiw, Tyr, and Tyw. Tuesday is a powerful day for workings that are related to accomplishment, achievement, action, aggression, anger, assertiveness, athletics, battle, beginnings, business, combustion, competition(s), conflict(s), confrontation(s), conquest, contests, courage, cutting, death, debate(s), destination, determination, drive, education, endurance, energy, enthusiasm, excitement, guns, hunting, independence, integrity, lawsuits, leadership, legality, logic, marriage, might, mortality, partnership, passion, politics, power, protection, purification, repairs, sports, strength, strife, tools, victory, violence, vitality, war, weapons, woodworking, youth, fast action, higher learning, male activities, male fertility, male goals, male rituals, mechanical things, new beginnings, physical action, physical competition(s), police matters, rapid movement, sexual love, power over enemies, strength in conflict, the honor code, and things that need to be done quickly.

With respect to people, it is an auspicious day for workings that are related to athletes, carpenters, competitors, contestants, debaters, drivers, enthusiasts, hunters, lawyers, mechanics, partners, politicians, soldiers, surgeons, warriors, businesspeople, police officers, woodworkers, and young people. It is also a day to overcome enemies, or move openly against enemies. Geographically, Tuesday is a great day for workings that are related to battlefields, courtrooms, pastures, trees, dry land, police stations, and sports arenas.

In the body, it is appropriate for workings that are related to healing, lust, sex, surgery, muscular activity, physical energy, physical strength, the muscles, the thumbs, the solar-plexus chakra, and to make ill. It is also an auspicious day for workings to assert yourself, banish negativity, charge forward, control power, get ahead, raise armies, seek truth, take the initiative, and buy or sell animals.

Tuesday Correspondences

Mars/Fire/South/East/Male/Aries/Scorpio

Color: black, gray, orange, pink, red, white, yellow; red is the primary color

Number: 2, 3

Metal: iron, all metals

Charm: red garments, red garter, red yarn, weapons

Stone: aventurine, bloodstone, carnelian, pink or white coral, emerald, garnet, lodestone, ruby, star sapphire, pink tourmaline

Animal: black cat, goat, griffin, hart, horse, lion, peacock, stag

Plant: barley, caraway, carnation, cinnamon, cockscomb, cornflower, cowslip, cypress, daisy, false hellebore, fern, ginger, hellebore, hibiscus, holly, horsetail, kerm oak, lavender, red lentil, nutmeg, pepper, peppermint, pine, plantain, rue, tamarind, thyme, willowherb

Incense: bdellium, brimstone, cassia, cedar, cinnamon, cypress wood, dragon's blood, euphorbium gum, ginger, gum ammoniac, mint, patchouli, pine resin, sandalwood, thyme, wood aloes, all incense made from aromatic bark and wood

Goddess: Anath (Victorious Goddess), Arianrhod, Eris, Hathor, the Morrigan (Battle Raven), Ninlil (Majestic Lady), Shakti

God: Ares (Throng of War), El, Gwynn ap Nudd, Hermod, Hoenir,

Horus, Mars, Nergal, Ogma, Ogun (Lord of Iron), Porevit, Shango, Tuisco, Tyr

Evocation: Amabiel, Hyniel, Samael, Satael, satyrs

❦ Wednesday (Woden's Day)

Wednesday is named for the Norse god Odin. It is a powerful time for alchemy, astrology, divination (of the past, present, or future), magick, uncrossing, and for workings that are related to accounting, advertising, alternatives, appointments, business, childhood, communication(s), computers, contracts, creativity, crossroads, cunning, editing, education, eloquence, experiments, intelligence, journalism, knowledge, language(s), law, learning, logic, memory, messages, money, music, patience, peace, perception(s), predictions, purposefulness, reflection, resourcefulness, reversal, science, self-expression, self-improvement, speed, study, thought, travel, understanding, wisdom, writing, higher education, mental action, mental clarity, mystical insight, phone calls, serious problems, the intellect, the mind, the seasons, visual arts, written communication, and the heavenly bodies.

With respect to people, it is an auspicious day for workings that are related to accountants, addicts, advertisers, artists, critics, editors, educators, intellectuals, journalists, merchants, musicians, neighbors, poets, relatives, scientists, siblings, students, teachers, travelers, writers, clerical workers, public speakers, visual artists, and young people. It is also a good day for workings to consult attorneys, hire employees, pacify judges, visit people, elevate the poor, and cast down the rich.

In the body, it is an appropriate time for workings that are related to addiction(s), celibacy, healing, medical matters, mental issues, and the throat chakra. Wednesday is also an auspicious day to plan magickal workings, and for workings to acquire metals, bind spirits, make plans, place ads, release spirits, sign contracts, win wars, open locks or bolts, surrender to divine will, and to wash your doorstep with inward motions at dawn in order to attract whatever you need.

Wednesday Correspondences

Color: black, light blue, brown, gray, green, magenta, orange, peach, purple, red, silver, turquoise, violet, white, yellow; orange is the primary color

Number: 3, 5

Metal: mercury ☠

Charm: distaff, rod, runes, staff, iridescent garments

Stone: moss agate, amethyst, bloodstone, emerald, hematite, lapis lazuli, lodestone, pearl, ruby, sapphire, sodalite, all blue stones

Animal: bear, dog, fox, magpie, swan, weasel

Plant: almond, bayberry, chamomile, cherry, cinnamon, cinquefoil, clove, coltsfoot, ginger, hazel, hazelnut, jasmine, lavender, millet, oak, peppermint, periwinkle, rosemary, sage, St. John's wort, sweet pea, tamarind, lemon verbena, violet

Incense: cassia, cedar, cinnamon, clove, frankincense, jasmine, lavender, mastic, mint, rosemary, sage, sandalwood, storax, dried and powdered citrus peel, and all incense made from aromatic bark, wood, and seeds

Goddess: Carmenta, Hecate (Queen of Crossroads), Hel, Ishtar, Ma'at, the Morrigan, Nike

God: Anubis, Bragi, Elath-Iahu, Enki, Garuda, Hermes, Maximon (Black Magician), Mercury, Nebo (Wise God of Wednesday), Odin, Shango, Ullr, Vishnu, Wayland, Woden

Evocation: Agrat Bat Mahalat, Michael, Miel, Raphael, Seraphiel, Tiriel

Thursday (Thor's day)

Thursday is named for the Norse thunder god. It is a powerful day for centering, lunar magick, weather magick, and workings that are related to beauty, broadcasting, business, charity, decisions, dedication, desires, ecstasy, employment, endurance, expansion, fidelity, forecasting, gambling, generosity, growth, harmony, honor(s), increase, justice, karma, law, logic, love, loyalty, luck, materialism, maturity, meetings, mercy, money, opportunity, philosophy, politics, poverty, prosperity, protection, psychology, publicity, publishing, reading, religion, research, riches, self-improvement, self-worth, speculation, sports, study, success, thunder, trade, treasure, truth, wealth, weddings, correspondence courses, court cases, financial matters, foreign affairs, good luck, good wishes, higher education, legal matters, male happiness, material success, material wealth, political power, social matters, spiritual progress, the lottery, and long distance travel.

With respect to people, it is a good day for workings that are related to broadcasters, doctors, employers, gamblers, guardians, merchants, philosophers, politicians, psychologists, publicists, publishers, researchers, thieves, traders, authority figures, and sports fans. It is also a powerful time for workings to appease enemies, attract love from women, and influence people in high places or who have power over you.

In the body, Thursday is appropriate for workings that are related to healing, health, male fertility, the brow chakra, and to banish depression. It is also an auspicious time for workings to banish negativity, ease strife, end quarrels, increase business, open doors, reach out, recoup losses, widen horizons, find or recover lost items, and attract more of what you already have. Thursday is considered a good day for a wedding if the couple wishes to have a lot of children.

Thursday Correspondences

Color: azure, blue, dark blue, royal blue, green, indigo, purple, royal purple, turquoise, violet, white, yellow, metallic colors; blue is the primary color

Number: 3, 4

Metal: tin

Charm: crown, sword, peacock feather, bright-blue garments, laurel crown with flowers

Stone: amethyst, carnelian, emerald, jade, lapis lazuli, peridot, sapphire, sugilite, tiger's-eye, turquoise

Animal: bull, cow, elephant, hart, horse, peacock, pigeon, ram, stag, stork, swallow

Plant: acorn, beech, birch, box, buttercup, calendula, chervil, cinnamon, fennel, heather, henbane ☠, ivy, laurel, lemon balm, lilac, nutmeg, oak, pepper, pistachio, pink rose, rye, saffron, stock, terebinth, turmeric, red water lily

Incense: ash keys, benzoin, cinnamon, clove, musk, nutmeg, saffron, sage, sandalwood, storax, wood aloes, and all aromatic fruits

Goddess: Asase Yaa, Oya

God: Aegir, Amon, Bel, Donar, Enlil, Forseti, Heimdall, Jupiter (Lord of the Sky), Ketu, Krishna, Marduk, Neptune, Njoerd, Nuadh, Perun (Lord of Thunder), Poseidon, Thor, Thunor, Zeus (Mighty Thunderer, Hurler of Lightning)

Evocation: Asasiel, Cassiel, Iophiel, Sachiel, Zachariel

❧ Friday (Freya's day)

Friday is named for the Norse goddess Freya. It is a powerful day for dream magick, flower magick, herbal magick, incense magick, and for workings that are related to activity, affairs, affection, alliances, appreciation, architecture, arousal, art, balance, beauty, change, competition(s), cosmetics, courage, courtship, creativity, dance, dating, decorating, design, disabilities, drawing, ease, emotions, engineering, enjoyment, entertainment, fashion, fertility, friendship, gardening, gentleness, gifts, glamor, grace, growth, harmony, income, love, luck, luxury, marriage, money, movement, music, painting, parties, partnership(s), passion, peace, perfume, pleasure, poetry, power, prosperity, reconciliation, relationships, relaxation, romance, sculpture, sensuality, sexuality, shopping, success, trees, understanding, union, vitality, artistic abilities, event planning, fairy dangers, female problems, female rituals, home improvements, inner beauty, intense emotions, interior decorating, material things, romantic love, social activities, and affairs of the heart.

This is a great day for workings that are related to people, especially architects, artists, chiropractors, contractors, dancers, designers, engineers, entertainers, friends, gardeners, lovers, musicians, painters, partners, poets, sculptors, event planners, hairstylists, handy persons, makeup artists, and soul mates. It is also a good day to encourage males to love females.

In the body, Friday is an appropriate time for workings that are related to healing, sex, physical healing, the heart chakra, and the uterus/ womb. It is also an auspicious day for workings to acquire silver, avert evil, encourage marriages, plan parties, quash dreams, attract luck or money, and set things in motion.

Friday Correspondences

Venus/Water/East/West/South/Dawn/Female/Libra/Taurus

Color: aqua, blue, light blue, brown, green, pale green, magenta, peach, pink, rose, white, all pastels

Number: 5, 6

Metal: copper

Charm: green or white garments, scepter

Stone: alexandrite, amethyst, coral, diamond, emerald, jade, jet, black moonstone, peridot, smoky quartz, tiger's-eye, pink tourmaline

Animal: camel, dove, elephant, goat, horse, pigeon, sparrow

Plant: apple, birch, cherry, clematis, clove, coriander, heather, hemlock, hibiscus, ivy, lotus, moss, myrtle, oats, pepperwort, peppermint, pine-cone, quince, raspberry, rose, pink rose, red rose, rose hips, saffron, sage, savin, stephanotis, strawberry, thyme, vanilla, verbena, violet, water lily, yarrow, and all flowers

Incense: ambergris, camphor, mace, musk, myrrh, rose, saffron, sage, sandalwood, sweetgrass, vanilla, violet, all floral scents

Goddess: Aphrodite, Asherah, Baalith, Brigid, Erzulie, Freya (Passionate Queen), Frigg, Gefion, Hathor (Beautiful One), Hestia, Inanna, Ishtar (Lady of Passion and Desire), Lakshmi, Lilith, Mokosh, Nehalennia, Nerthus, Ostara, Pombagira, Sarasvati, Shakti, Shekinah, Sirtur, Al Uzza, Venus (Queen of Pleasure), Vesta

God: Allah, Bacchus, Bes, Cupid, the Dagda, Dionysus, El, Eros (God of Love), Freyr, Frit Ailek, Shukra

Evocation: Agrat Bat Mahalat, Anael, Hagiel, Mokosha, Rashiel, Sachiel, Uriel, veelas

Saturday (Saturn-day)

Saturday is named for the Roman god Saturn. It is an auspicious day for meditation, spirit communication, and past-life work. It is also a power day for for magick, especially for averting, banishing, binding, containment, crossing, cursing, reversing, and workings that are related to authority, blocks, boundaries, building(s), career, caution, change, commitment, concentration, constriction(s), danger(s), death(s), debt(s), defense, discord, discovery, doctrines, duties, endings, endurance, fears, finances, freedom, funerals, houses, immobility, incarceration, inhibitions, institutions, investments, justice, karma, knowledge, laws, life, limitation(s), limits, longevity, maiming, manifestation, mathematics, money, motivation, murder, neutralization, obstacles, patience, peace, plumbing, prosecution, protection, reality, reincarnation, relaxation, repose, responsibilities, rules, sacrifice, self-esteem, self-discipline, separation(s), stability, structure(s), termination, tests, time, transformation, understanding, will, wisdom, work, hard work, karmic laws, lost items, material gain, negative thoughts, psychic ability, psychic self-defense, real estate, shared finances, the Zodiac, long-term conditions, and last wills and testaments.

With respect to people, this is a great day for workings that are related to criminals, dentists, families, murderers, plumbers, prosecutors, realtors, stalkers, civil servants, corrections officers, farm workers, funeral directors, missing persons, and the elderly. It is also a powerful time for workings to release the dead, bring someone to justice, locate missing persons, move secretly against enemies, overcome those who restrict you, and limit the freedom or the actions of others.

In the body, Saturday is appropriate for workings that are related to disabilities, the bones, the teeth, the root chakra, and to overcome diseases. It is also an auspicious day for workings to break free, cause problems, destroy pests, neutralize negativity, recognize limits, avert evil or negativity, find lost items, banish or bind negative forces or influences, and to overcome blockages, limitations, or obstacles.

Saturday Correspondences

Saturn/Pluto/Earth/North/Southwest/Female/Aquarius/Capricorn

Color: black, dark blue, dark brown, gray, dark gray, indigo, dark purple, red, white, yellow; black is the primary color

Number: 6, 7

Metal: lead ☠

Charm: black garments, crutch, hook, sickle

Stone: amethyst, carbon, diamond, labradorite, lava, lodestone, onyx, snowflake obsidian, pumice, smoky quartz, sapphire, turquoise

Animal: bat, black cat, crow, dragon, hog, owl, raven, tiger

Plant: alder, amaranth, basil, coltsfoot, corn, ebony, fir, hemlock, henbane ☠, hyacinth, iris, juniper, mallow, mandrake, moss, nightshade, black orchid, pansy, parsley, pepperwort, pomegranate, poppy seed, sesame seed, stinging nettle, thyme, lemon verbena, wolfbane ☠

Incense: brimstone, copal, frankincense, fumitory, ginger, ginseng, myrrh, patchouli, rosemary, and all incense made from aromatic roots

Goddess: Ceres, Cybele (Magna Mater), Demeter, Durga (Remover of Distress), Gaia, Hel, Holda (Mistress of the Dead), Nammu, Nana Buruku, the Norns, Oshun, Ran, Rhea (Great Mother), Skadi, Tellus, Vesta, Yemaya

God: Baron Samedi (Baron Saturday), Bran, Cronos, the Dagda, El (Master of Time), Hades, Herne (the Hunter), Jehovah (Lord of the Sabbath), Lava Ailek, Loki, Mimir, Ninib, Ninurta, Odin, Osiris (Lord of Eternity), Pan, Pluto, Saturn (Father Time), Seater, Set, Shani

Evocation: Agiel, Cassiel, Machatan, Orifiel, Uriel

Hours

The hours of both the day and the night are each ruled by a planet, making them powerful times for specific workings.

✧ Sun

The Sun rules the first hour after sunrise on Sunday, and the first hour after sunset on Wednesday. These are power times for divination, pathworking, male magick, seasonal magick, solar magick, Fire magick/rituals/spells, and workings that are related to achievement, action, activation, activity, advancement, agriculture, arrogance, attraction, authority, awakening, bigotry, bioenergy, brilliance, charisma, cheerfulness, confidence, connection, consciousness, courage, creation, creativity, defense, dignity, dominance, dryness, ego, energy, enlightenment, ethics, expansion, fame, fatherhood, favor(s), fertility, fire(s), force, fortune, friendship, gardening, glory, goals, greed, government, growth, happiness, heat, heritage, honor(s), hope, illumination, immortality, improvement, inheritance, invincibility, joy, justice, laughter, law, leadership, life, light, maturity, morality, movement, opening, optimism, passage, perception, positiveness, power, pride, promotion, prosperity, protection, rebirth, regeneration, return, rulership, self-confidence, stability, stimulation, strength, success, travel, victory, vitality, warmth, wealth, well-being, will, willpower, wisdom, work, yang, abstract spirit, auspicious beginnings, creative power, divine energy, divine right, financial gain, healing energy, healing power, legal matters, magickal energy, natural power, night travel, omnipresent knowledge, personal fulfillment, physical energy, positive energy, projective energy, pure spirit, rapid growth, sexual energy, solar blessings, solar energy, solar power, the God, the intellect, the positive, total success, upward movement, fertility of land, fertility of Nature, fertility of plants, generosity of spirit, male vital spirits, the conscious mind, the god power, the life force, the performing arts, the power of light, the urge for power, and the brilliance of the intellect.

These are also power hours to awaken understanding, banish negativity, detect evil, end enmity, nourish plants, preserve life, raise power, win awards, witness oaths, end legal matters, heal with light, increase ritual energy, avert or banish darkness, help a garden grow, purify crystals, objects, or stones; overcome darkness, death, or personal pride; attract blessings, gods, honors, money, or yang; and to activate change, crystals, fertility, or the potential of a new day.

With respect to people, these are auspicious times for workings that are related to bigots, CEOs, children, fathers, gentlemen, hunters, husbands, leaders, men, metalworkers, noblemen, potentates, royalty, rulers, sultans, superiors, authority figures, mint workers, performance artists, and local government officials. In terms of structures, these are power hours for workings that are related to halls, houses, mansions, palaces, theaters, dining rooms, great rooms, and all grand buildings that are in habitable condition. In the business world, these are auspicious times for workings that are related to authority, banking, careers, mints, business ethics, and everything from the previous section that applies to business, such as goals, promotion, success, and financial gain.

In the body, these are powerful times for workings that are related to acne, cramps, fainting, fevers, healing, health, tremors, virility, bad breath, bone marrow, brain diseases, eye problems, good health, heart disease, mouth diseases, seasonal depression, the back, the brain, the eyes (especially the left eyes of women, and the right eyes of men), the heart (especially in males), the joints, the male brain, and discharges from the eyes. They are also auspicious times for workings to energize chakras, improve depression, and protect against diseases and disorders.

Sun Correspondences

Sun/Fire/East/West/Noon/Day/Sunday/Male/Leo

Color: gold, orange, red, scarlet, purple, white, yellow

Number: 1, 4, 6, 7, 8, 21, 111

Metal: brass, copper, gold

Element: antimony, sulfur

Stone: red agate, amber, golden beryl, orange calcite, blood-red carbuncle, carnelian, chrysoberyl, chrysolite, chrysoprase, citrine, diamond, yellow diamond, heliodor, jacinth, lodestone, peridot, pipestone, pyrite, clear quartz crystal, ruby, sunstone, tiger's-eye, topaz, zircon

Charm: child, disk, egg, gold ring, honey, musk, prism, scepter, wheel

Animal: baboon, beetle, scarab beetle, boar, buffalo, bull, crocodile, eagle, falcon, firefly, hawk, white horse, lion, lizard, oyster, phoenix, ram, rooster, seal, sea snail, sphinx, starfish, swan, vulture, spotted wolf, all shellfish, all phosphorescent creatures

Plant: acacia, amber, angelica, ash, balm, barley, beech, birch, bistort, broom, burnet, butterbur, buttercup, calamus, carnation, clove carnation, cascara sagrada, cassia, cedar, celandine, centaury, chamomile, cinnamon, cinquefoil, citron, clove, cowslip, dittany of Crete, elecampane, everlasting, eyebright, galangal, gentian, ginger, ginseng, grapevine, gum arabic, hazel, Helen's flower, heliotrope, hibiscus, hollyhock, hops, ivy, juniper, knotgrass, laurel, lemon, lotus, lovage, marigold, marjoram, marsh mallow, mint, mistletoe, oak, orange, palm, peony, black pepper, raspberry, rosemary, rowan, rue, saffron, smartweed, spikenard, St. John's wort, sundew, sunflower, tangerine, tormentil, vervain, viper's bugloss, walnut, zedoary, all citrus fruits and the trees that bear them

Incense: amber, benzoin, cedar, cinnamon, clove, copal, frankincense, juniper, mastic, musk, myrrh, olibanum, patchouli, rosemary, sandalwood, wood aloes

Goddess: Adsulatta, Aega, Aimend, Akewa, Alectrona, Allat, Amaterasu Omikami (Heaven-Radiant Great Divinity), Aphrodite Asteria (of the Sun), Arinna, Asva, Aya, Bast (in lion form), Bisal-Mariamna, Brigid, Chup-Kamui, Coatlicue, Eos, Gnowee, Graine (House of the Sun), Hathor (Golden One, Eye of Ra), Hebat, Hepat, Hsi-Ho, Igaehindvo, Isis (Shining One, Ray of the Sun), Mallina, Mor, Ningal, Saule, Sekhmet (Powerful One, The One Who Shines in the Sky), Selqet, Shams, Shapash (Eternal Sun, Torch of the Gods), Sunna (Mistress Sun), Tamar, Teteoinnan, Walo, Wuriupranili, Yhi

God: Abraxas, Agni, Ah Kinchil, Ahau Kin, Akycha, Amon, Amon-Ra, Angpetu Wi, Aodh, Apollo, Apollo Belenus, Ard Greimme, Aton, Atum, Baal (He Who Mounts the Clouds), Baal Phegor, Babbar, Baldur, Bel (Shining One), Belenus (Brilliant One), Bladud, Bochicha, Cautha, Dazhbog, Freyr, Gwawl, Heliogabalus, Helios, Horus (High One, Lord of Heaven, Horus of the Horizon), Huitzilopochtli, Hyperion, Indra, Inti, Kephera, Khors, Kinich Ahau, Krishna, Lisa, Lucifer (Bringer of Light, Son of Morning), Lugh (Shining One), Marduk, Maui, Mithras (Light of Heaven, Light of the World, Lord of Heavenly Light), Mitra (Lord of Day), Ogma (Sun Face), Pautiwa, Phoebus Apollo, Ra (Lord of Heaven), Rama, Sabazius, Savitar, Shakuru, Shamash (Judge of the Heavens), Sol, Surya (Most Resplendent One, The Thousand-Rayed, Illuminator of Infinite Causes), Sutalidihi, Tankun, Tezcatlipoca, Tonatiuh, Tsohanoai

Evocation: Chur, the Heliades (Daughters of the Sun), Herakles Ogmius, Hercules Melkarth, Michael, Raphael, Samson, Semeliel, Zerachiel

Moon

The Moon rules the first hour after sunrise on Monday, and the first hour after sunset on Thursday. These are power times for divination, enchantment, magick, meditation, witchcraft, astral projection, calendar magick, cauldron spells, dream work, female magick, inner work, lunar magick, night magick, psychic work, triple magick, sea rituals/spells, Water magick/rituals/spells, and for workings that are related to balance, birth, calm, changeability, change(s), clairvoyance, compassion, consciousness, creativity, cycles, danger, deceit, delusion, dreams, emotions, envy, family, fascination, femininity, fertility, fluidity, gardening, generation, growth, guidance, hexes, hunting, illumination, illusion, imagination, imbalance, increase, influence, inspiration, instincts, intuition, irrationality, jealousy, joy, light, liquidity, love, maternity, misfortune, moisture, moods, motherhood, movement, navigation, negativity, nightmares, passage, peace, personality, poetry, pregnancy, rain, rebirth, reincarnation, return, secrets, self-renewal, shadows, sleep, sloth, sorrow, spells, spirituality, sympathy, theft, tides, time, tranquility, transformation, travel (especially at night or by water), yin, circular time, clear mind, creative inspiration, divination tools, domestic matters, emotional well-being, evil thoughts, female Mysteries, inner wisdom, lunar wisdom, magickal power(s), maternal love, negative emotions, ocean voyages, pooled water, prophetic dreams, psychic awareness, psychic development, psychic dreams, psychic power(s), psychic sensitivity, rapid speech, receptive energy, spiritual connections, spiritual growth, the feminine, the home, the moist, the nocturnal, the subconscious, triple power, watery things, women's work, measurement of time, passage of time, the unconscious mind, willingness to change, inner eye of wisdom, the cycle of life, the mysteries of time, the power of light, and the call of the wild. These are also power hours for workings to reduce anxiety, solve problems, begin anything new, increase psychic abilities, overcome creative blocks, activate crystals or fertility, calm down your life, improve attitude or memory, open to lunar magick, purify stones, objects, or crystals, and to attract yin or the Goddess.

With respect to people, these are auspicious times for workings that are related to babies, children, commoners, drivers, fisherfolk, hunters, ladies, magicians, mariners, messengers midwives, mothers, noblewomen, nurses, pilgrims, queens, sailors, travelers, vagabonds, viziers, witches, women, cleaning people, delivery people, executive assistants, fish merchants, letter carriers, chiefs of staff, female street vendors, those who make or sell alcoholic beverages, and all those who work on or with water. They are also good times to protect children and travelers.

In the business world, these are power hours for workings that are related to bars, taverns, merchandise, cleaning services, delivery services, livery services, maritime trade, messenger services, and fish farms/markets/shops. Geographically, these are auspicious hours for workings that are related to baths, bogs, brooks, fields, fountains, highways, lakes, oceans, ponds, pools, ports, rivers, seas, shores, springs, waterways, and all bodies of water.

In the body, these are powerful times for workings that are related to abscesses, addiction, alcoholics, anxiety, cancer, childbirth, cold(s), convulsions, coughs, cysts, edema, epilepsy, fat, fertility, gout, growth, healing, measles, menstruation, mucus, jaundice, obesity, overindulgence, palsy, paralysis, rheumatism, seizures, sciatica, smallpox, strokes, sweat, tears, bodily fluids, eye injuries (especially to the left eyes of males and the right eyes of females), female fertility, female genitals, kidney stones, menstrual disorders, menstrual pain/cramps, mental illness, mood swings, reproductive organs, running sores, stomach aches, the bladder, the brain, the breasts, the eyes, the glands, the head, the intestines, the liver (especially in females), the lungs, the pancreas, the spine, the stomach, wasting diseases, the uterus/womb, brain diseases/disorders, female reproductive system, neurological diseases/disorders, relapsing/recurrent fever, the left eye, the lymphatic system, the menstrual cycle, the left side of men, the right side of women, and infirmities caused by cold moisture.

Moon Correspondences

Moon (all phases)/Water/Night/Monday/Female/Cancer

Color: pale blue, gray, pale green, silver, white, pale pearlescent shades, pale yellowish white

Number: 2, 3, 6, 7, 8, 9, 13, 14, 50, 369

Metal: silver

Stone: aquamarine, beryl, sea-green beryl, clear calcite, chalcedony, emerald, fluorspar, gypsum, labradorite, marcasite, moonstone, mother-of-pearl, white opal, pearl, clear quartz crystal, sapphire, white sapphire, sea salt, selenite, tiger's-eye, turquoise; all soft stones; all green stones; all white stones

Charm: silver, white or yellow ball, cheese, coconut milk, cow horns, silver crescent, egg whites, hunting horn, milk, menstrual blood, white shells, spear, tree sap, all silver objects

Animal: baboon, bat, scarab beetle, white bull, cat, chameleon, civet cat, cockle, cow, coyote, crab, crane, dog, dolphin, duck, elephant, frog, goat, goose, grebe, hare, heron, hind, horse, ibis, mouse, nightingale, otter, oyster, panther, rabbit, seal, serpent, sparrow, stag, suckerfish, swine, toad, tortoise, vixen, wolf, wryneck; all amphibians, all nocturnal creatures, all water fowl, and all birds that sing at night

Plant: acanthus, adder's tongue, agave, aloe, anise, arrowhead vine, banana, barley, bat nut, bergamot, bladderwrack, blessed thistle, breadfruit, burnet saxifrage, cabbage, calamus, camellia, carob, cascarilla, cedar, chamomile, chaste tree, chickweed, cleavers, club moss, coconut, coralwort, cotton, cuckoo flower, cucumber, cyclamen, daisy, duckweed, dulse, endive, eucalyptus, fennel, fluellen, forget-me-not, gardenia, garlic, ginseng, grape, hawkweed, hawthorn, hazel, honeysuckle, hyacinth, hyssop, iris, jacaranda, jasmine, kale, laburnum, lemon, lemon balm, lemongrass, lettuce, lily,

lily of the valley, linden, loosestrife, lotus, madonna lily, mallow, mandrake, mango, mesquite, mimosa, moonflower, moonwort, mouse-eared hawkweed, mugwort, myrtle, narcissus, nutmeg, olive, onion, orpine, opium poppy ☠, orache, orris root, palm, papaya, passionflower, pea, peach, wild pear, pellitory, peony, periwinkle, poppy, poppy seed, potato, privet, pumpkin, purslane, queen of the night, rattlegrass, rhubarb, dog rose, white rose, wild rose, rosemary, clary sage, saxifrage, sea holly, seaweed, sedum, sorrel, star anise, stonecrop, trefoil, turnip, turmeric, veronica, vervain, vetch, wallflower, watercress, water lily, willow, wintergreen, wormwood, yam, ylang-ylang, yucca; all gourds, melons, squash, aquatic plants, leafy vegetables, resinous or succulent plants, and night-blooming flowers

Fungus: mushrooms, psylocibe mushroom ☠, all fungi

Incense: amber, camphor, coconut, galbanum, ginseng, jasmine, lotus, myrrh, olibanum, sandalwood, wood aloes, ylang-ylang

Goddess: Aine, Alcmene, Alcyone, Allat, Alphito, Anumati, Anunitu, Aradia, Arianrhod (Silver Wheel), Artemis, Artemis Callisto, Asherah, Asherali, Ashima, Ashtoreth, Astarte, Atargatis, Auchimolgen, Aya, Baalith, Bast (in cat form), Belili, Bendis, Blodeuwedd, Britomartis, Brizo, Calliope, Callisto, Cameira, Candi, Ceres, Cerridwen, Chang-O (Queen Moon), Circe, Coatlicue, Coyolxauhqui (Golden Bells), Danu, Dewi Shri, Diana (Queen of the Night), Diana Lucifera (Bringer of Light), Dictynna, Durga, Erzulie, Erzulie Freda, Estsanatlehi (Changing Woman), Eurynome, Fatima, Freya, Frigg, the Goddess, Hanwi (Grandmother Moon), Hathor, Hecate (Queen of the Night), Hecate Selene (Far-Shooting Moon), Helice, Hera, Hina, Ialysa, Ina, Inanna (Queen Moon), Ishtar, Isis, Ix Chel, Jana, Jarah, Jezanna, Juno, Juno Luna, Kilya, Latona, Leucothea, Linda, Losna, Lucina, Luna, Luonnotar, Lupa, Mama Quilla (Mother Moon), Manasa-Devi, Mawu, Ngame, Ningal, Noctiluca (She Who Is Awake at Night), Nut, Perimbó, Phoebe (Shining Brightly), Prosperine, Rhiannon, Selene (The Radiant), Sheng Mu, Tanith, Ursula,

Venus, Wahini-Hai (The Moon), the White Goddess, Xochiquetzal, Yemaya, Yolkai Estsan, Zarpanit, Zirna

God: Ai-ada, 'Amm, Aningan, As-im-babbar, Bahloo, Chandra, Coniraya, El, Eterah, Geyaguga, Gou, Hanghepi Wi, Hubal, Iah, Igaluk, Ilmaqah, Kashku, Khonsu (The Wanderer, He Who Traverses the Sky), Kusuh, Lisa, Metztli, Il Mukah, Myesyats, Nanna, Nyamiabe, Osiris, Pah, Phorcys, Poseidon, Shiva, Shiva Somantha (Lord of the Moon), Sin (Illuminator, Lord of the Calendar), Soma, Suen, Tarqeq, Thoth, Tsuki-Yomi, Varuna, Wadd, Yarikh (Lamp of Heaven), Yue-Lao (Moon Elder, Old Man in the Moon)

Evocation: Elimiel, Gabriel, the Hyades, Iaqwiel, Ichadriel, Io, Nimuë, Pasiphaë (She Who Shines for All), Phaedra, Porphyrion, Tsaphiel, Yahriel, Zachariel

Mars

Mars rules the first hour after sunrise on Tuesday, and the first hour after sunset on Friday. These are power times for banishing, grounding, aggressive magick, battlefield magick, dragon magick, male sex magick, Fire magick/rituals/spells, and workings that are related to action, aggression, aggressiveness, ambition, anger, assertiveness, attack, battle, beginnings, birth, boldness, competition(s), conflict(s), courage, defense, desire(s), destruction, determination, discord, disharmony, drive, endurance, energy, engineering, enmity, exorcism, force, goals, growth, hardness, initiative, machinery, marriage, passion, politics, power, protection, quarrels, recklessness, sports, strength, strife, struggle, terrorism, upheaval, victory, violence, war, warfare, will, work, yang, aggressive action, angry passion, assertive action, blood lust, emotional passion, law enforcement, male Mysteries, male rituals, male sexuality, physical skill(s), police matters, positive energy, projective energy, rapid speech, sexual advances, sexual energy, the masculine, violent death, violent temper, and the ability to fight. These are also power hours for workings to fight, assert yourself, send energy, overcome psychic attack, and use energy to fight.

With respect to people, these are auspicious times for workings that are related to athletes, bakers, barbers, butchers, carpenters, chefs, competitors, dentists, doctors, enemies, engineers, executioners, fighters, generals, machinists, men, pharmacists, sergeants, soldiers, surgeons, tailors, terrorists, tyrants, warriors, court officers, law enforcers, police officers, the middle-aged, high-ranking military officers, and all those who make fire or use drills, weapons, or cutting tools in their work. They are also good times for workings to defeat enemies.

In the body, these are powerful times for workings that are related to blisters, fevers, libido, lust, ringworm, sex, surgery, broken veins, choleric diseases, chronic fever, fungal infections, male genitals, medical issues, migraine headaches, physical energy, physical strength, premature birth, the muscles, the testicles, the left ear, and the right nostril. They are also auspicious times for workings to heal after surgery.

Mars Correspondences (Planetary)

Mars/Fire/East/South/Right/Tuesday/Night/Male/Aries/Scorpio

Color: green, orange, red

Number: 1, 2, 3, 4, 5, 9, 16, 65

Metal: brass, iron, steel

Element: sulfur

Stone: amethyst, bloodstone, diamond, flint, garnet, jasper, red jasper, lava, lodestone, magnetite, obsidian, onyx, pipestone, rhodochrosite, rhodonite, ruby, pyrite, sard, sardonyx, tiger's-eye, red or watermelon tourmaline; rocks formed from more than one kind of stone

Charm: battle-ax, helmet, musk, spear, sword, all weapons

Animal: wild ass, baboon, beta fish, crow, fire-breathing dragon, eagle, falcon, fly, gnat, baby goat, hawk, horse, jackdaw, kestrel, kite, leopard, magpie, mule, horned owl, screech owl, pike, ram, raven, sturgeon, swordfish, vulture, wolf, woodpecker; all birds of prey and poisonous snakes

Plant: aloe, all-heal, allspice, anemone, arbutus, arrowroot, asafetida, asarabacca, ash, avens, barberry, basil, betony, black cohosh, blessed thistle, bloodroot ☠, box, broom, broomrape, bryony, butcher's broom, cactus, caper, carnation, carrot, cattail, cayenne, cedar, chili pepper, chives, coffee, coriander, cow parsnip, cuckoopint, cumin, daisy, damiana, dandelion, dead nettle, deerstongue, dogwood, dwarf elder, dyer's broom, euphorbium, everlasting, eye of Satan ☠, figwort, flax, galangal, garlic, gentian, geranium, ginger, gorse, grains of paradise, gum ammoniac, hawthorn, hellebore, herb Robert, hickory, High John, holly, holly oak, honeysuckle, hops, horseradish, houndstongue, jalapeño pepper, laurel, leek, red lentil, Low John, madder root, maguey, marsh buttercup, masterwort, mezereon, mountain ash, mustard, mustard seed, nettle, Norfolk Island pine, onion, paprika, parsley, passionflower, pennyroyal, pepper, peppermint, pimento, pine, plantain (herb), poke root, radish, reed, restharrow, rhubarb, dog rose, wild rose, rowan, rue, rye, sarsaparilla, savin, scallion, scammony, senna, shallot, snapdragon, spurge laurel, star thistle, self-heal, squill, sulphurwort, tarragon, thistle, toadflax, tobacco ☠, tormentil, turmeric, valerian, Venus flytrap, vervain, vetiver, wolfbane ☠, woodruff, wormwood, yucca; all hallucinogens ☠, every kind of scented wood, all plants that are prickly, thorny, or inflame the skin, and any plant that tastes bitter or tart, or burns the tongue, or provokes tears

Fungus: all hallucinogenic fungi ☠

Incense: ambergris, benzoin, cedar, dragon's blood, frankincense, ginger, labdanum, mastic, musk, opoponax, pine resin, sandalwood, storax, wood aloes; all gum resins and fragrant woods

Goddess: Anahita, Anath (the Destroyer), Aparajita (the Unconquered), Ashtoreth (Lady of Horses and Chariots), Astarte, Athena, Badb (the Fury, Raven of Battle), Bellona, Brigid, Durga (Slayer of Demons), Epona, Eris, Fea (the Hateful), Inanna, Ishtar (Lady of Battle, Queen of Attack and Hand-to-Hand Fighting), Macha, Maeve, Medb, Minerva, the Morrigan, Nana, Neith (Mistress of the Bow and Ruler of the Arrows), Nemain, Nematona, Oya, Rhiannon, Sekhmet (the Warrior, She Who Overcomes All Enemies), the Valkyries

God: Amon, Ares, Ashur, Belatucadros, Camulos, Cocidus (The Red One), Esus, Huitzilopochtli, Indra, Jehovah Melkarth, Karttikeya, Lugal-Irra, Lugh, Mangala, Marduk, Mars, Melicertes, Melkarth, Mithras, Nergal, Ninurta, Nodens, Nuadh, Odin, Ogou-Feraille, Ogun, Perun, Quirinus, Reshep, Set (the Red God), Shango, Teutates, Thor, Tyr, Vahagan

Evocation: Amabiel, Hercules Melkarth, Madimiel, Samael

✑ Mercury

Mercury rules the first hour after sunrise on Wednesday, and the first hour after sunset on Saturday. These are power times for divination, magick, voice magick, Air magick/rituals/spells, and for workings that are related to adaptability, alertness, business, change, cleverness, cognition, communication (all forms), contracts, correspondence, creativity, crossroads, debt(s), deceit, deception, dexterity, discovery, dishonesty, duality, eloquence, falsehood, fear(s), finances, gambling, gymnastics, humor, ideas, inconstancy, industry, information, ingenuity, inspiration, intelligence, interpretation, learning, love, mathematics, memory, messages, money, nervousness, perception, prophecy, quickness, rebirth, science, self-improvement, skill, speech, speed, study, teaching, thievery, thought, travel (all conveyances), trickiness, Trickster energy, vagabondage, vehemence, wealth, wisdom, wrestling, writing, fast talking, intellectual workings, magickal power(s), mental abilities, mental power(s), mood swings, occult power(s), quick wit, the media, the occult, and the wisdom of rebirth. These are also power hours to break negative habits, and protect against theft.

In the business world, these are auspicious hours for workings that are related to commerce, contracts, purchasing, sales, business transactions, and everything listed above that can relate to business, such as correspondence, debt(s), finances, and money. With respect to people, these are good times for workings that are related to children, comedians, gamblers, gymnasts, industrialists, interpreters, mathematicians, scientists, scribes, teachers, telemarketers, thieves, ventriloquists, wrestlers, writers, businesspeople, and con artists. They are also good times for workings to protect against thieves.

In the body, these are powerful times for workings that are related to breathing, cures, depression, mental illness, healing, epilepsy, memory, the brain, the hands, the lungs, the mind, the mouth, the nerves, the thighs, the tongue, and the respiratory system. They are also appropriate times for workings to overcome addictions and speed healing.

Mercury Correspondences (Planetary)

Mercury/Air/Water/North/Wednesday/Gemini/Virgo

Color: blue, bronze, copper, gold, orange, purple, silver, violet, yellow, white; metallics, mixtures of colors

Number: 1, 4, 5, 6, 7, 8, 10, 260

Metal: aluminum, mercury ☿, tin, zinc, all alloys

Stone: agate, amber, amethyst, aquamarine, aventurine, chalcedony, chrysolite, diamond, emerald, jade, jasper, mottled jasper, red marble, marcasite, mica, opal, fire opal, peridot, pumice, serpentine, smoky quartz, tiger's-eye, topaz; artificial stones, and natural stones of more than one color

Charm: caduceus, hermaphrodite, twins

Animal: ape, black beetle, blackbird, blue jay, chameleon, civet cat, clownfish, coyote, dog, earthworm, finch, fox, hare, hart, hyena, ibis, jackal, lapwing, lark, linnet, magpie, monkey, mule, mullet, nightingale, parrot, rabbit, raven, sea anemone, twin serpents, thrush, weasel, wolverine, all songbirds, and all creatures that can change their appearance or their gender, or which use deception to survive

Plant: acacia, almond, angelica, anise, ash, aspen, azalea, bamboo, basil, bayberry, bean, bergamot, bittersweet, bracken, Brazil nut, buckbean, butterbur, calamint, caraway, cardamom, carrot, cascara sagrada, cassia, celery, chicory, cinnamon, cinquefoil, clove, clover, coltsfoot, coriander seed, cornflower, costmary, cow parsnip, devil's-bit scabious, dill, endive, elecampane, eucalyptus, fennel, fenugreek, fern, filbert, flax, foxglove, fumitory, garlic mustard, germander, gum arabic, hazel, hazelnut, hedge mustard, High John, honeysuckle, horehound, hound's tongue, iris, Jacob's ladder, jasmine, lavender, lavender cotton, lemongrass, lemon peel, licorice, lilac, lily of the valley, linden, lungwort, mace, magnolia, maidenhair fern, mandrake, American mandrake, marjoram, mercury, mint, mistletoe, mulberry, mullein, myrtle, nailwort, oat, oregano, papyrus, parsley, parsnip, pecan, pellitory, pennyroyal, peppermint, peyote cactus ☠, pimpernel, pistachio, pomegranate, rosemary, clary sage, savory, scullcap, self-heal, senna, southernwood, snapdragon, spearmint, star anise, stillengia, storax, sweet pea, tansy, thyme, valerian, lemon verbena, vervain, vetiver, woodbine, woody nightshade; all variegrated plants, all fragrant seeds, and plants that bloom and produce seeds but do not bear fruit

Fungus: fly agaric ☠

Incense: benzoin, galbanum, lavender, mastic, mint, nutmeg, rosemary, sandalwood, spikenard, storax; all bark and seeds that can be burned as incense

Goddess: Athena, Carmenta, Carya, Frigg, Gefion, Inanna, Isis, Ma'at, Maia, Metis, Minerva, Pombagira, Sheela-na-gig

God: Abarta, Anansi, Angra Mainyu, Anubis, Arawn, Bluejay, Cernunnos, the Dagda, Ea, Enki, Esus, Ganesha, Great Hare, Gwydion, Hermes, Herne, Kokopelli, Konira Viracocha, Krishna, Kutnahin, Legba, Loki, Lugh, Maui (of the Thousand Tricks), Maximon, Mercury, Moccus, Nabu, Odin, Prometheus, Qat, Q're, Raven, Serapis, Tezcatlipoca, Thor, Thoth, Ueuecoyotl (Coyote), Vishnu

Evocation: Barkiel, Br'er Rabbit, Buddha, Devil/Shaitan, Hasdiel, High John the Conqueror, leprechauns, manitou, Medusa, Michael, Sir Palamedes, Raphael, Reynard the Fox, Sun Hou-Tzu, Tiriel, Ulysses/Odysseus, Zadkiel

🐦 Jupiter

Jupiter rules the first hour after sunrise on Thursday, and the first hour after sunset on Sunday. These are power times for meditation, psychic work, Air magick/rituals/spells, Fire magick/rituals/spells, and workings that are related to abundance, apparel, authority, benevolence, business, control, deities, devoutness, dignity, education, excesses, expansion, fame, favor, gambling, generosity, grandeur, gravitas, greed, growth, honor(s), increase, influence, intellect, intuition, joviality, justice, kindness, law, leadership, luck, luxury, marriage, might, money, nourishment, optimism, parties, philosophy, politics, power, pride, prosperity, religion, reputation, responsibility, riches, rulership, satisfaction, self-reinforcement, spirituality, stateliness, success, visions, wastefulness, wealth, wisdom, good fortune, higher education, lawful gains, legal problems, material goods, political victory, power bases, public acclaim, things desired, powers that be, the higher mind, and the vital force. These are also appropriate times for workings to acquire wealth, attract prosperity, banish anxiety, create sympathy, and settle legal matters.

In the business world, these are powerful times for workings that are related to commercial transactions and financial speculation, and to create prosperity, grow a business, expand an enterprise, or settle legal problems. With respect to people, these are good times for workings that are related to elders, executives, intellectuals, judges, kings, leaders, philosophers, politicians, rulers, royalty, authority figures, power brokers, religious leaders, and those who have fame or influence. They are also great times for workings to encourage friendships and protect travelers.

In the body, these are auspicious times for workings that are related to apoplexy, cramps, digestion, headaches, heartburn, nutrition, pleurisy, sperm, virility, glandular diseases, lung infections, dental problems, major headaches, the abdomen, the blood, the cartilage, the glands, the liver, the lungs, the ribs, blood diseases/disorders, the digestive system, and the left ear. They are also great times for workings to preserve health.

Jupiter Correspondences (Planetary)

Jupiter/Air/Fire/East/Day/Thursday/Sagittarius/Pisces

Color: blue, dark blue, royal blue, green, lilac, magenta, mauve, purple, royal purple

Number: 3, 4, 5, 7, 9, 22, 34

Metal: gold, silver, tin

Stone: amethyst, beryl, chrysolite, diamond, emerald, jacinth, jasper, green jasper, lapis lazuli, lepidolite, sapphire, sugilite, topaz, turquoise

Charm: arrow, ash key, baton, egg yolk, raisin, sugar, thunderbolt, olive oil

Animal: anchovy, cuckoo, dolphin, eagle, elephant, hart, hen, lamb, partridge, pelican, pheasant, seal, sheath fish, sheep, stork, swallow, thunderbird, unicorn

Plant: agrimony, almond, anise, apple, apricot, arnica, ash, asparagus, avens, balm of Gilead, banyan, barley, basil, beech, white beet, belleric, bergamot, betony, bilberry, birch, blood root ☠, blueberry, bodhi tree, borage, brooklime, carnation, clove carnation, carrageen, cedar, celandine, centaury, chervil, chestnut, chicory, cinnamon, cinquefoil, clove, clover, red clover, coltsfoot, costmary, couch grass, cypress, dandelion, darnel, dock, dogwood, elecampane, emblic, endive, fennel, fig, filbert, flax, gentian, ginger, ginseng, goldenseal, grapevine, hart's tongue, hazel, heliotrope, henbane ☠, hickory, holly, honeysuckle, horse chestnut, houseleek, hyssop, Indian plum, Irish moss, jasmine, Chinese juniper, juniper berry, laurel, lavender, lemon balm, licorice, linden, lungwort, mace, madder, magnolia, maple tree, marsh mallow, marsh woundwort, masterwort, mastic, meadowsweet, melilot, milk thistle, mint, mistletoe, mulberry, mullein, nutmeg, nuts, oak, oakmoss, oats, olive tree, orris root, pear, peepul, peony root, scarlet pimpernel, pine, pineapple, pistachio, plum, polypody, poplar, opium poppy ☠, raspberry, rhubarb, red rose, saffron, sage, samphire, sarsaparilla, sassafras, scurvy grass, sorb apple, sorrel, star anise, sugarcane, sycamore, tamarisk, tansy, terebinth, ti, tomato, tonka bean, unicorn root, vanilla, violet, viper's bugloss, wallflower, walnut tree, wheat, witchgrass; trees that bear fruit but do not produce flowers, and plants that taste astringent, pleasant, or sweet

Incense: amber, ambergris, cedar, cinnamon, clove, fumitory, ginger, jasmine, mastic, myrrh, nutmeg, pine resin, sage, sandalwood, storax, vanilla

Goddess: Anath (Lady of Heaven, Ruler of Dominion), Athena, Danu (Mother of the Gods), Devi (Universal Mother), Hathor (Great Mother of the World), Hera (Queen of Heaven), Isis (Mistress of the Sky, Queen of the Universe), Juno (Queen of Heaven), Nut (Mystery of Heaven), Oya, Satis, Shakti, Themis, Unial, Victoria

God: Adad (Lord of the Sky), Ahura Mazda, Akongo, Allah, Amon, Anu (King of Heaven, Father of the Gods), Baal (The Thunderer), Baal Shamin (Lord of the Skies, Bearer of Thunder) Bel, Brihaspati, the Dagda (Great Father), Devapurohita, Dis Pater (Father of the Gods), Dushares, Dyaus (Sky Father), El, Gwydion, Horagalles, Indra (God of the Blue

Vault), Ishkur (Lord Who Rides the Storm), Itzamna, Jehovah, Jupiter (Thunderer, King of Heaven), Jupiter Ammon, Marduk (Thrower of Thunderbolts), Nuadh (Cloud-Maker), Odin (All-Father), Ogma, Perkunas, Perun (the Striker, Lord of Thunder), Reshep, Rimmon (The Thunderer), Shango, Sky Father, Taranis, Telamon, Teshub (Lord of Heaven), Thor (Lord of Thunder), Tinia, Ukko, Viracocha, Wadd, Yahweh, Zanahary (Father of Heaven), Zeus (All-Father, Lord of Thunderbolts, Master of the Bright Lightning)

Evocation: Adabiel, Barchiel, Hercules, Imdugud, Sachiel, Zachariel, Zadkiel

❧ Venus

Venus rules the first hour after sunrise on Friday and the first hour after sunset on Monday. These are power times for meditation, garden magick, incense magick, mirror magick, female sex magick, Water magick/rituals/spells, and workings that are related to affection, amorousness, art, attraction, attractiveness, beauty, business, compassion, connection, contracts, courtship, creativity, desire, elegance, fellowship, fertility, friendship, frivolity, gardening, happiness, harmony, indulgence, interchanges, isolation, joy, kindness, leisure, love, luck, luxury, marriage, money, music, partnership(s), passion, peacefulness, pilgrimage, pleasure, receptivity, reconciliation, relationships, relaxation, return, romance, scent, seduction, sensuality, sex, sexuality, society, sweetness, yin, youth, abstract emotions, auspicious beginnings, female genitals, female rituals, female sexuality, married love, personal income, personal finances, profane love, receptive energy, sacred promiscuity, sacred prostitution, sensual passion, sexual advances, sexual energy, sexual love, sexual power, social matters, the feminine, visual arts, the power of love, and initiation into the mysteries of love. These are also power hours to energize spells and for workings to lead on, and attract affection, love, lust, or prosperity.

With respect to people, these are power hours for workings that are related to adolescents, children, composers, friends, lovers, musicians, partners, pilgrims, spouses, strangers, women, visual artists, and young people. In the body, these are auspicious times for workings that are related to healing, health, kundalini, lechery, lust, phlegm, semen, sex, colds/flu, physical love, physical passion, sexual healing, sexual need, sexual passion, sexual union, the blood, the buttocks, the flanks, the heart, the kidneys, the liver, the pelvis, the stomach, the thumb, the throat, the veins, the yoni, the left nostril, the womb/uterus, sexually transmitted diseases, and reproductive system diseases/disorders. It's also a great time for workings to satisfy lust.

Venus Correspondences (Planetary)
Venus/Earth/Water/West/Friday/Midnight/Taurus/Libra

Color: blue, green (all shades), emerald green, indigo, pink, rose; with green primary

Number: 3, 4, 5, 6, 7, 33, 72, 175

Metal: brass, copper, silver

Stone: aetite, amber, amethyst, aventurine, azurite, beryl, pink or blue or green calcite, carnelian, chrysocolla, chrysolite, chrysoprase, coral, emerald, jade, green jasper, kunzite, lapis lazuli, lodestone, malachite, morganite, olivine, opal, pearl, peridot, rose quartz, sapphire, sodalite, tiger's-eye, blue or green or pink or watermelon tourmaline, turquoise; all green stones

Charm: almond oil, ambergris, conch shell, cowry shell, hand mirror, honey, olive oil, palmarosa, pentacle, perfume, pod or bud, sugar

Animal: bull, calf, crab, crow, dog, dove, eagle, gilthead bream, goat, hare, lynx, pelican, Emperor penguin, pigeon, rabbit, sardine, sheep, sheldrake, swallow, swan, turtledove, wagtail, whiting; all creatures that have high sex drives, or behave very lovingly toward their young

Plant: acacia flowers, Adam and Eve root, African violet, alder, black alder, alfalfa, alkanet, aloe, amaranth, ambrosia, angelica, apple, apricot, artichoke, ash, asphodel, aster, avocado, bachelor's buttons, balm of Gilead, banana, barley, basil, beans, beech, bergamot, betony, birch, bishop's weed, bleeding heart, bramble, buckwheat, bugle, burdock, cape gooseberry, caper, cardamom, carnation, catnip, catsfoot, lesser celandine, chamomile, cherry, chestnut, chickpea, cinchona, coltsfoot, columbine, coriander, corn, cowslip, crocus, cudweed, cuckoo flower, cyclamen, daffodil, daisy, damiana, datura ☠, devil's-bit scabious, dittany of Crete, dropwort, elder, eryngo, feverfew, fig, figwort, foxglove, red foxglove, freesia, gardenia, geranium, rose geranium, goldenrod, gooseberry, gromwell, ground ivy, groundsel, hawthorn, heather, herb Paris, herb Robert, hibiscus, huckleberry, hyacinth, Indian paintbrush, iris, jasmine, kidneywort, ladies' bedstraw, lady's mantle, larkspur, laurel, lavender, licorice, lilac, lily of the valley, linden, lobster claw, lucky hand, magnolia, maidenhair fern, mallow, marsh mallow, meadowsweet, mercury, mint, moneywort, motherwort, mugwort, myrtle, narcissus, navelwort, oats, orache, orris, orchid, pansy, parsley piert, parsnip, passionflower, pea, peach, pear, pennyroyal, peppermint, periwinkle, plantain (herb), plum, plumeria, pomegranate, poppy, primrose, privet, purslane, quince, ragwort, raspberry, rose, damask rose, wild rose, rye, saffron, sage, sagebrush, sanicle, sea-blite, sea holly, self-heal, silverweed, soapwort, soap plant, sorrel, sow thistle, spearmint, spider lily, spignel, stephanotis, strawberry, sugarcane, sweet pea, sycamore, tansy, teasel, thyme, wild thyme, tomato, tonka bean, tuberose, tulip, valerian, vanilla, Venus flytrap, Venus's looking glass, lemon verbena, vervain, vetiver, violet, wheat, willow, wormwood, yarrow, ylang-ylang, yohimbine; all plants that taste sweet, all fragrant flowers, and all plants that produce flowers and seeds but do not bear fruit

Incense: benzoin, camphor, civet, dragon's blood, jasmine, labdanum, mint, musk, myrrh, rose, sandalwood, storax, sweetgrass, thyme, vanilla, violet, wood aloes

Goddess: Aega, Allat, Anahita, Anath, Anunitu, Aphrodite, Asherah, Ashtoreth, Astarte, Atargatis, Baalat, Bast, Belili, Belit, Belit-Ilani, Beltis, Branwen (Venus of the Northern Seas), Britomartis, Chasca, Dilbah (She Who Opens the Heavens in Her Supremacy), Fatima, Freya, Frigg, Gendenwitha (the Morning Star), Geshtinanna, Hathor, Inanna, Ishtar (Star of Heaven, Bright Light of Nights), Isis, Lakshmi, Maeve, Medb, Mylitta, Ninlil, Oshun, Qadesh, Rati, Rhea, Shaushka, Tethys, Tlazolteotl, Turan, Al Uzza (Venus of Mecca), Venus, Zib, Zorya Utrennyaya (Aurora of the Morning), Zorya Vechernyaya (Aurora of the Evening)

God: Adonis, Angus, Arsu (Evening Star), the Asvins, 'Athtar, Azizos (Morning Star), Bel, Cupid, Dionysus, Eros (Evening Star), Lucifer (Son of Morning, Bringer of Light), Oceanus, Pan, Phaëthon, Phosphoros, Quetzalcoatl, Salem (Evening Star), Shaharu, Shalemu, Shukra, Tlaloc, Tlauixcalpantecuhtli, the Usins, Xolotl (Lord of the Evening Star)

Evocation: Anael (Angel of the Star of Love), Haniel, Hasdiel, Mab, Mary Magdalene, Raphael, Robin Hood

❧ Saturn

Saturn rules the first hour after sunrise on Saturday and the first hour after sunset on Tuesday. These are power times for astral work, banishing, binding, centering, grounding, hexing, uncrossing, Water magick/rituals/spells, and workings that are related to agriculture, ambition, archaeology, architecture, austerity, authority, building, business, caution, civilization, cold, conservatism, consolidation, control, darkness, death, debt(s), decrepitude, defense, delay(s), discipline, dissolution, doctrines, eldership, endings, endurance, exorcism, fear, history, inflexibility, inhibition, institutions, karma, knowledge, laziness, lessons, limitation(s), loneliness, longevity, losses, loyalty, luck, meanness, melancholy, mining, misery, morality, mutation, obstacles, obstruction, oppression, patience, peace, politics, practicality, profundity, protection, prudence, purification, reliability, responsibility, restriction(s), ruins, sadness, sobriety, solitude, sorrow, spiritualism, stability, structure(s), sorrow, tediousness, temperance, time, wisdom, vision, concrete mind, hidden treasure, karmic debts, magickal knowledge, old age, other planes, psychic defense, sacred wisdom, slow movement, social order, strength through persistence and endurance, the permanent continuation of things, and things that are obtained with difficulty or after long journeys.

These are also power hours for workings to achieve goals, banish harm, limit freedom, receive blessings, set limits, stop gossip, bind negative forces, end bad habits, increase psychic awareness, win a quarrel, protect against conspiracy, negativity, or poisoning, and to work out karma through evolution.

With respect to people, these are power hours for workings that are related to architects, archaeologists, bankers, conservatives, disciplinarians, elders, fathers, grandparents, historians, jailers, miners, monks, treasurers, depressed people, and the elderly (especially old men). They are also great times to bring someone to justice and limit the actions of others.

In the business world, they are appropriate times for workings that are related to property deals and real estate, especially banks, buildings, land, and farmland. In the body, these are auspicious times for workings that are related to aging, arthritis, depression, osteoporosis, pain, tears, abscessed teeth, the bones, the gallbladder, the joints, the ligaments, the skeleton, the skin, the teeth, the tendons, tooth decay, the pituitary gland, the reproductive glands, the right ear, and bone damage/diseases/disorders. They are also great times for workings to overcome lust or chronic pain.

Saturn Correspondences (Planetary)

Saturn/Water/Earth/West/Center/Left/Saturday/Day/Capricorn/Aquarius

Color: black, blue, dark blue, dark brown, gray, cool green, indigo; with black primary

Number: 2, 3, 7, 8, 10, 15, 22

Metal: gold, iron, lead ♄, steel

Element: alum, sulfur

Stone: Apache tear, azurite, carnelian, chalcedony, coal, diamond, garnet, hematite, ironstone, brown jasper, jet, lodestone, marcasite, obsidian, onyx, pearl, ruby, salt, sapphire, black star sapphire, serpentine, black tourmaline; all black stones

Charm: civet, crutch, sickle, black objects, anything from the Earth that is dark and heavy

Animal: adder, ant, ape, ass, basilisk, bat, bear, buffalo, camel, cat, cockle, black cow, crane, crow, dogfish, dragon, eel, fox, hare, hog, lamprey, lapwing, mole, mouse, mule, horned owl, screech owl, oyster, peacock, quail, raven, ostrich, scorpion, sloth, snake, sea sponge, toad, tortoise, wolf, wren; all vermin, black animals, nocturnal creatures, solitary animals, and all creatures that crawl or creep; animals that eat their young or have other disgusting feeding habits, and birds with long necks or harsh voices

Plant: alder, amaranth, asafetida, aspen, asphodel, balm of Gilead, barley, beech, red beet, field beet, belladonna, birch, bishop's weed, bistort, blackthorn, boneset, buckthorn, burdock, cannabis, caraway, cassia, centaury, chickweed, cockle, comfrey, coriander, Indian corn, cornflower, cumin, cypress, daffodil, darnel, datura ☠, dodder, dogwood, ebony, black elder, elm, eryngo, euphorbia, eye of Satan ☠, fenugreek, fern, black fig, fir, fleawort, fluxweed, foxglove, guaiacum wood, hawkweed, hawthorn, hellebore, black hellebore, hemlock, water hemlock, henbane ☠, High John, holly, horsetail, houseleek, hyacinth, gladwin iris, ironwood, ivy, kava kava, knapweed, knotgrass, lady's slipper, all white lilies, lobelia, love-lies-bleeding, Low John, Madonna lily, male fern, mandrake, masterwort, medlar, melancholy thistle, mimosa, morning glory, moss, mullein, nightshade, oleander, onion, black orchid, pansy, pine, opium poppy, pansy, pepperwort, periwinkle, pine, plantain (herb), polypody, pomegranate, poplar, quince, rowan, royal fern, rue, rupturewort, rye, scammony, scullcap, senna, service tree, shepherd's purse, skunk cabbage, slippery elm, snowdrop, Solomon's seal, spleenwort, squill, tamarind, tamarisk, thyme, thoroughwort, tobacco ☠, twyblade, valerian, violet, wall fern, weeping willow, willowherb, wintergreen, witch hazel, woad, wolfbane ☠, yew; all roots, dead plants, poisonous plants, unpleasant-smelling plants, and very old plants and trees; anything that grows in the ruins of houses or in stagnant water or from other putrefaction; plants that cast dark shadows, produce black fruit, or taste sour or bitter; plants and trees that cause stupefaction, never bear fruit, or bear fruit but do not produce flowers

Fungus: Jew's ear

Incense: benzoin, brimstone, frankincense, fumitory, musk, myrrh, patchouli, sandalwood, spikenard

Goddess: Aditi (Eternal Space), Allat, Amba, Anahita, Ariadne, Ceres, Cybele, Demeter, Durga, Ereshkigal, the Great Goddess, Hathor, Hecate, Hera, Isis (Lady of Eternity), Juno, Kali (Black Time, Mighty Time), Nephthys, Ops, Pandora, Rhea, Satis, Sekhmet, Sesheta (Minister of Time), Shakti, Sophia, Ushas (Mistress of Time)

God: Ahura Mazda, Allah, Amon (Lord of Time), Angus, Baal, Baal Shamin, Bran, Cronos, the Dagda, El (Master of Time), Jehovah, Kalki, Khonsu, Krishna, Kumarbi, Kurma, Maha-Kala (Great Time), Matsya, Moloch, Ninib, Ninurta, Osiris (Lord of Eternity), Ra, Sani, Saturn (Father Time), Shiva, Thor, Thoth, Uranus, Vishnu, Yahweh, Yama, Yu-Huang-Shang-Ti (Father Heaven, the August Supreme Emperor of Jade), Zurvan (Boundless Time)

Evocation: Buddha, Cassiel, Father Time, John Barleycorn, Maion, Methuselah, Michael, Orifiel, Zaphkiel

Tables of Planetary Hours

I have never had the patience to follow this, but perhaps you do. An almanac or other authoritative source is needed to determine the exact times of sunrise and sunset for each day of the year. Starting from those points, you take the daytime and nighttime hours and divide them by twelve to determine the time periods that are ruled by each planet. Except on the Spring and Autumn Equinoxes, the "hours" will not be sixty minutes long.

Just thinking about this gives me a headache, but if you have more patience and better math skills than I do, you can work it out. These traditional charts can be used to further empower your magick, as outlined in the preceding material.

Table 1. Planetary Hours from Sunrise

Hour	Sunday	Monday	Tuesday	Wednesday	Thursday	Friday	Saturday
1st	Sun	Moon	Mars	Mercury	Jupiter	Venus	Saturn
2nd	Venus	Saturn	Sun	Moon	Mars	Mercury	Jupiter
3rd	Mercury	Jupiter	Venus	Saturn	Sun	Moon	Mars
4th	Moon	Mars	Mercury	Jupiter	Venus	Saturn	Sun
5th	Saturn	Sun	Moon	Mars	Mercury	Jupiter	Venus
6th	Jupiter	Venus	Saturn	Sun	Moon	Mars	Mercury
7th	Mars	Mercury	Jupiter	Venus	Saturn	Sun	Moon
8th	Sun	Moon	Mars	Mercury	Jupiter	Venus	Saturn
9th	Venus	Saturn	Sun	Moon	Mars	Mercury	Jupiter
10th	Mercury	Jupiter	Venus	Saturn	Sun	Moon	Mars
11th	Moon	Mars	Mercury	Jupiter	Venus	Saturn	Sun
12th	Saturn	Sun	Moon	Mars	Mercury	Jupiter	Venus

Table 2. Planetary Hours from Sunset

Hour	Sunday	Monday	Tuesday	Wednesday	Thursday	Friday	Saturday
1st	Jupiter	Venus	Saturn	Sun	Moon	Mars	Mercury
2nd	Mars	Mercury	Jupiter	Venus	Saturn	Sun	Moon
3rd	Sun	Moon	Mars	Mercury	Jupiter	Venus	Saturn
4th	Venus	Saturn	Sun	Moon	Mars	Mercury	Jupiter
5th	Mercury	Jupiter	Venus	Saturn	Sun	Moon	Mars
6th	Moon	Mars	Mercury	Jupiter	Venus	Saturn	Sun
7th	Saturn	Sun	Moon	Mars	Mercury	Jupiter	Venus
8th	Jupiter	Venus	Saturn	Sun	Moon	Mars	Mercury
9th	Mars	Mercury	Jupiter	Venus	Saturn	Sun	Moon
10th	Sun	Moon	Mars	Mercury	Jupiter	Venus	Saturn
11th	Venus	Saturn	Sun	Moon	Mars	Mercury	Jupiter
12th	Mercury	Jupiter	Venus	Saturn	Sun	Moon	Mars

PART THREE

Other Cycles

THE PLANETARY BODIES that we can most easily observe and experience are the Moon and Sun. They are fixtures in our sky, so we cannot help but notice their movements or feel their effects. Everyone has seen the Moon and been warmed by the Sun. Even those with no sense of wonder have been enchanted by moonbeams, moved by the beauty of moonlight sparkling on water, or filled with hope or joy when storm clouds parted and slants of sunlight revealed an arching rainbow.

Consider, then, how powerfully lunar and solar energies can be wielded by practioners who are sensitive to them. To work white magick is to weave light. Use the information in this section of the book to boost the success of your workings with lunar or solar power.

Lunar Cycles

The Moon follows a regular cycle of 28 days every lunar month, and the wise practitioner makes strategic use of that in magick. There are two ways to do this. The first is simple, the second more esoteric, but they both work. The simple method is to regard the Moon as having three phases (Waxing, Full, Waning) and to work magick accordingly, as outlined below. The second method further categorizes the Moon's phases, counts the days, and provides additional opportunities for specific workings, as also outlined below.

You can use either method, a combination of the two, or even disregard the Moon altogether in deciding when to cast your spells, make magickal things, or hold your rituals. This is for you to decide, as is how you feel about working magick during the Dark Moon, or when the Moon is void of course.

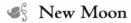 New Moon

(also called Balsamic Moon;
the first three days that the Moon becomes visible)

When the Lady's Moon is new,
Kiss thy hand to Her times two.
—REDE OF THE WICCAE[1]

The New Moon is a powerful time for meditation, raising, reclaiming, reflecting, releasing, and for workings that are related to agriculture, beauty, beginnings, birth, career, compassion, forgiveness, gardening, growth, healing, health, hunting, increase, initiation, joy, love, networking, optimism, rebirth, reflection, rejuvenation, renewal, romance, self-improvement, speech, stability, transformation, virginity, weddings, cyclical rebeginning, erotic dreams, fresh starts, new friendships, new ideas, new partnerships, new projects, new relationships, new ventures, personal growth, surreptitious advantage, states of ignorance, and clarity leading to wisdom.

The New Moon is also an auspicious time to begin workings that will take a long time to complete, and for workings to attract love, buy animals, destroy lies, end strife, make plans, begin anything new, consecrate new tools, find a job, create a shield of protection, and get a new angle on a problem.

New Moon Correspondences

New Moon/East/North/Day/Spring

Color: black, pink, silver, white

Plant: yew

---

1. This version of "Rede of the Wiccae" has been passed on by Lady Gwen, who received it from her grandmother, Adriana Porter. From "Wicca-Pagan Port-Pourri" in *Green Egg*, Vol. VIII, no. 69, spring 1975, p. 10.

Goddess: Artemis, Athena, Brigid, Clotho, Ishtar, Isis, Juno, the Kotharat, Kuhu, Lakshmi, Linda, the Maiden, Mary, Ninhursag, Prosymna, Sadarnuna, Selene, the White Goddess

God: An, Apollo Noumenios, As-im-babbar, Hillel, Khonsu, Osiris

Evocation: Aerope, Agathos Daimon, Antiope, Chrysaor, Elektra, Nimuë

⚘ Waxing Crescent Moon

(the third to seventh days after the New Moon)

The horns of the Moon face left during the Waxing Crescent Moon. It is a powerful time for animal magick and workings that are related to beginning(s), birth, business, change, emotions, flow, goals, increase, initiative, momentum, opening, organization, possibilities, matriarchal strength, and wisdom leading to illumination. It is also an auspicious time to launch ships; move house; protect babies, cows, and nursing mothers; and to return evil to its sender or source.

Waxing Crescent Moon Correspondences

Crescent Moon/East/Day/Spring

Color: gold, orange, silver, white

Metal: gold, silver

Charm: archery bow, crescent, gold or silver crescent moon, horn(s), milk, sickle, tall hat or staff surmounted by a crescent moon or with solar disk and crescent moon

Animal: white bull, cat, white cow, dolphin

Plant: white rose

Goddess: Allat, Anahita (Immaculate One), Artemis (Maiden Huntress), Astarte, Atargatis, Diana, Hera, Lalita, the Maiden, Matangi, Qadesh (Lady of the Stars of Heaven), Sarasvati, Shodashi, Tana, Tanith, Tiamat, Tlazolteotl, and Aphrodite, Ishtar, Isis (She of Green Wings and Crescent Moon), Mary, Venus, and Yemaya, especially in their aspect of Stella Maris (Star of the Sea)

God: Aglibol, Allah, 'Amm, Cernunnos, Crom Cruach (Blood Crescent), Herne, Hillel, Ilumquh, Khonsu (He Who Traverses the Sky), Nanna, Qos, Shiva, Sin (Lord of the Diadem), Suen, Thoth, Wadd, Yarikh (Lord of the Sickle)

Evocation: merfolk, Nimuë

✺ Waxing Moon

(also called First Quarter Moon; the seventh to tenth days after the New Moon)

Deosil go by the waxing Moon—
Sing and dance the Wiccan rune.
—Rede of the Wiccae

The Waxing Moon is a powerful time for invocation, unbinding, deosil magick, elemental magick, Earth magick/rituals/spells, and constructive workings that are related to abundance, attraction, beauty, beginning(s), birth, continuity, couples, courage, empathy, fertility, friendship, fulfillment, gain, growth, healing, health, ideas, increase, inspiration (strongest when the Moon is nearly full), intensity, knowledge, love, luck, money, motivation, prosperity, protection, sensuality, success, wealth, well-being, creative energy, good fortune, good health, healing power, new beginnings, passionate creativity, pleasure trips, positive changes, psychic awareness, psychic increase, the body, the physical, and young women.

It is also an auspicious time to attract, begin, charge, consecrate, improve, increase, invite, sow, strengthen, and overcome, such as in workings to attract good luck, begin spells, charge talismans, consecrate candles, improve health, increase money, invite love, overcome obstacles, sow seeds, and strengthen relationships. Magickal plants are traditionally harvested during the Waxing Moon, and it is a good time to cut hair to encourage growth.

Waxing Moon Correspondences

Waxing Moon/Earth/East/Sunset/Spring

Color: black, green, red, silver, white

Goddess: Artemis, Diana, Epona, Lalita, the Lalita Nityas, the Maiden, Neith, Ri, Shodashi

Gibbous Moon

(also called Waxing Gibbous Moon; the tenth to thirteenth days after the New Moon)

The Gibbous Moon is a powerful time for workings that are related to growth, increase, patience, solutions, and new ideas. It is also an auspicious time to perfect, and to work toward goals.

Gibbous Moon Correspondences

See Waxing Moon

✑ Full Moon

(technically the fourteenth day after the New Moon, but most practitioners include the day before and after as well)

When *the Moon rides at Her peak*
Then your heart's desire seek.
—REDE OF THE WICCAE

The Full Moon is the time of maximum magickal power, when an abundance of magickal energy is available to strengthen the effectiveness of spells and rituals. It is an auspicious time for divination, invocation, scrying, unbinding, dream work, psychic work, and every type of magick, especially cauldron spells, coven work, lunar magick, and workings that are related to action, alertness, beauty, certainty, change, clarity, competition(s), creation, creativity, culmination, decisions, dreams, emotions, energy, enlightenment, fecundity, fulfillment, growth, harvest, illumination, inspiration, knowledge, light, love, manifestation, maturity, money, motivation, need, nurture, plans, potency, power, prophecy, prosperity, protection, purification, relationships, romance, sacrifice, self-improvement, self-knowledge, sexuality, strength, transformation, travel, understanding, wisdom, artistic projects, inner knowledge, inner wisdom, legal matters, lunar power, magickal power(s), prophetic dreams, psychic ability, psychic energy, sacred knowledge, serious matters, and the mind.

With respect to people, the Full Moon is a great time for workings that are related to children, lovers, mothers, psychics, family members, and pregnant women. In the body, it is an appropriate time for workings that are related to fertility, healing, health, menstruation, pregnancy, sex, and mental illness. It is also a good time to heal serious illnesses.

This is a powerful time to attain, attract, complete, find, gain, increase, satisfy, search, share, and solve, such as workings to attain goals, attract money, complete projects, find jobs, get what you need, increase psychic ability, satisfy needs, share knowledge, and solve problems. The Full Moon is also the best time to empower spells, remove hexes, face hard facts, use will properly, meditate on your motives, see things through to their ends, and work with the Goddess. Cutting your hair during the Full Moon can make it thicker.

Full Moon Correspondences
Full Moon/South/Midnight/Night/Summer

Color: green, red, silver, white, deep yellow

Metal: silver

Charm: amphiphontes (round white cake studded with lit candles), cauldron, circle, egg, menstrual blood, scarab, silver objects, white turban

Animal: white cat, coyote, crayfish, dog, wolf

Plant: white carnation, gardenia, hawthorn, jasmine, mandrake, white mulberry

Fungus: mushroom

Incense: benzoin, camphor, frankincense, jasmine, myrrh, sandalwood

Goddess: Anumati, Arianrhod (Silver Wheel), Artemis Mounykhia, Astarte, Calliope (Beauteous Face), Cameira, Danu, Diana, the Errinyes, Freya, Isis (Goddess Fifteen), Isis Selene, Juno (Queen of Heaven), Juno Luna, Losna, Luna, Maia, the Mother, Nemesis, Phoebe (Bright Moon), Selene (The Radiant, Bright-dressed Queen), Yemaya

God: Horkos, Jupiter (Shining Father), Odin, Osiris, Father Nanna, Nanna-Sin, Sin (The Illuminator), Thor

Evocation: dryads, Iphigenia, Mary Magdalene, Medusa, mermaids, nereids, nymphs, Pammon, Pasiphaë (She Who Shines for All), Praxithea, Rhode, werewolves

✒ Monthly Full Moons

Each Full Moon has its own unique character, making it helpful for specific magickal and metaphysical workings.

The names, from various cultures and traditions, are very much based on local climate and weather conditions. Most of them come from Europe and North America, so there will be places on this planet where they will not apply at all. Many of the names are assigned to more than one month, to reflect local climate and weather conditions.

January's Full Moon

Names for January's Full Moon include Birch Moon (12/24–1/20), Chaste Moon, Cold Moon, Cooking Moon, Disting Moon, Goose Moon, Great Spirit Moon, Holiday Moon, Ice Moon, Moon after Yule, Moon of Beginning, Moon of Inception, Moon of Little Winter, Old Moon, Quiet Moon, Snow Moon, Terrible Moon, Winter Moon, and Wolf Moon.

This is a powerful time for workings that are related to beginning(s), birth, children, creativity, protection, purification, quiet, rebirth, reversal, survival, and personal problems. It is also an auspicious time to gather together around the hearth for warmth, work magick for protection, and to keep the wolf (poverty) away from the door. Depending on where you live, it may also be a good time for ice magick and snow magick.

February's Full Moon

Names for February's Full Moon include Big Winter Moon, Bony Moon, Budding or Budding Time or Opening Buds Moon, Chaste Moon, Cleansing Moon, Elder Moon, Horning Moon, Hunger Moon, Ice Moon or Moon of Ice, Little Famine Moon, Moon of Popping Trees, Moon of Vision, Quickening Moon, Raccoon Moon, Red Moon, Rowan Moon (1/21–2/17), Snow Moon, Storm Moon, Trapper's Moon, Wild Moon, and Wolf Moon.

This is a powerful time for banishing, clairvoyance, clearing, divination, astral projection, vision quests, Air magick/rituals/spells, and workings that are related to elders, empowerment, guidance, healing, purification, purity, quickening, self-guidance, self-respect, spirituality, storms, wholeness, vision, and your future. Depending on where you live, it can also be an auspicious time for ice magick, snow magick, weather magick, or workings that are related to emergence, growth, or survival.

March's Full Moon

Names for March's Full Moon include Ash Moon (2/18–3/17), Big Famine Moon, Chaste Moon, Crow Moon, Crust Moon, Fish Moon, Lenten or Lenting Moon, Maple Sugar or Sugaring Moon, Moon of Ice, Moon of Waters, Moon of Winds or Windy Moon, Moon of the Snowblind, Plow Moon, Sap Moon, Seed Moon, Sleepy Moon, Storm Moon, and Worm Moon.

This is a powerful time for every kind of magick, but especially workings that are related to balance, exploration, healing, love, prosperity, protection, renewal, storms, new beginnings, spiritual knowledge, and the intellect. This is also an auspicious time for workings to break illusions and see truth. Depending on where you live, it can also be a good time for seed magick, weather magick, wind spells, or workings that are related to fertility, rising, survival, or thawing.

April's Full Moon

Names for April's Full Moon include Alder Moon (3/18–4/14), Awakening Moon, Budding Trees Moon, Egg Moon, Fish Moon, Flower Moon, Frog Moon, Grass or Sprouting Grass or Green Grass Moon, Growing Moon, Hare Moon, Moon When Geese Return, Ostara Moon, Peony Moon, Pink Moon, Planting or Planter's Moon, Red Grass Moon, Seed Moon, Wildcat Moon, and Wind Moon.

This is a powerful time for workings that are related to awakening, change, defense, duty, fertility, growth, peace, prosperity, self-confidence, self-guidance, self-reliance, selfishness, spirituality, teaching, wholeness, and mental prowess. Depending on where you live, it can also be an auspicious time for flower magick, seed magick, weather magick, wind spells, or workings that are related to emergence.

May's Full Moon

Names for May's Full Moon include Bright Moon, Budding Moon, Corn Planting Moon, Dragon Moon, Dyad Moon, Flower Moon, Frogs Return Moon, Grass Moon, Hare Moon, Hawthorn Moon (5/13–6/9), Merry Moon or Merrymoon, Milk Moon, Moon When Leaves Are Green, Moon When Ponies Shed, Panther Moon, Planting Moon, Willow Moon (4/15–5/12), and Witches' Moon.

This is a powerful time for binding, dragon magick, dream work, fairy magick, female magick, flower magick, positive magick, seed magick, sex magick, tree magick, Earth magick/rituals/spells, every kind of witchcraft, and workings that are related to balance, couples, creativity, emergence, fertility, goals, happiness, healing, intuition, joy, love, partners, peace, prosperity, protection, and sleep.

June's Full Moon

Names for June's Full Moon include Bear Moon, Dyad Moon, Fallow Moon, Flower Moon, Green Corn Moon, Honey Moon, Lotus Moon, Lovers' Moon, Mead Moon, Moon before Litha, Moon of Horses, Moon of Making Fat, Moon When Berries Are Ripe, Oak Moon (6/10–7/7), Planting Moon, Rose Moon, Strawberry Moon, Strong Sun Moon, and Windy Moon.

This is a powerful time for binding, animal magick, flower magick, inner work, male magick, positive magick, psychic work, and workings that are related to couples, endurance, fertility, fidelity, lovers, partners, polarity, prophecy, prosperity, protection, security, self-control, sex, strength, twins, male Mysteries, and personal responsibility. Depending on where you live, it may also be an auspicious time for wind spells.

July's Full Moon

Names for July's Full Moon include Blessing Moon, Blood Moon or Moon of Blood, Buck Moon, Crane Moon, Fallow Moon, Hay Moon, Holly Moon (7/8–8/4), Hungry Ghost Moon, Mead Moon, Moon of Claiming, Moon of Middle Summer, Moon of the Wise, Ripe Corn Moon, Rose Moon, Summer Moon, Thunder Moon, and Wort Moon.

This is a powerful time for binding, divination, meditation, animal magick, dream work, positive magick, psychic work, and workings that are related to blessing(s), courage, fertility, manifestation, polarity, potency, prophecy, protection, security, sex magick, strength, success, wisdom, and spiritual goals. Depending on where you live, it may also be an auspicious time for wortcraft, or weather magick.

August's Full Moon

Names for August's Full Moon include Barley Moon, Corn Moon, Dispute Moon, Dog Day's Moon, Fruit Moon, Grain Moon, Green Corn Moon or Moon of the Green Corn, Harvest Moon, Hazel Moon (8/5–9/I), Lightning Moon, Moon of Celebration, Moon When All Things Ripen, Moon When Cherries Turn Black, Red Moon, Sturgeon Moon, Women's Moon, and Wort or Wyrt Moon.

This is a powerful time for divination, dowsing, meditation, wildcrafting, wortcraft, animal magick, herbal magick, spirit work, and workings that are related to appreciation, eternity, fertility, friendship, gathering, healing, inspiration, manifestation, polarity, preservation, prophecy, prosperity, protection, ripening, spirituality, and vitality.

September's Full Moon

Names for September's Full Moon include Barley Moon, Chrysanthemum Moon, Crone Moon, Fruit Moon, Harvest Moon, Moon of the Wise, Moon When Calves Grow Hair, Moon When Deer Paw the Earth, Mulberry Moon, Nut Moon, Shedding Moon, Singing Moon, Sturgeon Moon, Vine Moon (9/2–9/29), and Wine Moon.

This is a powerful time for banishing, clearing, Crone magick, Earth magick/rituals/spells, and workings that are related to balance, cooperation, fertility, flexibility, healing, manifestation, organization, protection, sex, thanksgiving, wisdom, and psychic development. Depending on where you live, this may also be an auspicious time for workings that are related to gathering and harvest.

October's Full Moon

Name's for October's Full Moon include Beaver Moon, Blackberry Moon, Blood Moon, Falling Leaf Moon or Moon of Falling Leaves, Frosty Moon, Harvest Moon, Hearth Moon, Hunter's or Hunting Moon, Ivy Moon (9/30–10/27), Kindly Moon, Moon of the Changing Season, Moon of the Home or House, Moon of Truth, Moon When Quilling and Beading Is Done, Sanguine Moon, Shedding Moon, Ten Colds Moon, Wine Moon, and Winter Moon.

This is a powerful time for banishing, binding, releasing, hearth magick, spirit communication, spirit work, and workings that are related to balance, change, cooperation, courage, fertility, flexibility, healing, hunting, inspiration, justice, karma, kindness, love, prosperity, protection, reincarnation, sacrifice, spirituality, thanksgiving, truth, inner harmony, and family matters. It is also an auspicious time for crafts, and for workings to make ready for Winter, to protect the home, and to release things that no longer serve you well.

November's Full Moon

Names for November's Full Moon include Ancestor Moon, Beaver Moon, Cold Moon, Dark Moon, Fog Moon, Frost or Frosty Moon, Hearth Moon, Hunter's or Hunting Moon, Long Nights Moon, Mad Moon, Moon before Yule, Moon of Beginning, Moon of the Dead, Moon of Inception, Moon of Storms, Moon When Deer Shed Antlers, Moon When Horses Are Broken Off, Mourning Moon, Reed Moon (10/28–11/24), Sassafras Moon, Snow Moon, Trading Moon, and Tree Moon.

It is a powerful time for banishing, cloaking, invocation, hearth magick, inner work, and for workings that are related to beginnings, cooperation, creativity, fertility, flexibility, healing, hunting, love, preparation(s), protection, purification, sacrifice, storms, trade, transformation, trust, truth, family matters, and spiritual progress. It is also an auspicious time for workings to banish negative thoughts, clear negative vibrations, protect children, and work with ancestors. Depending on where you live, this may also be a good time for weather magick.

December's Full Moon

Names for December's Full Moon include Bear Moon, Baby Bear Moon, Big Winter Moon, Bitter Moon, Christmas Moon, Cold Moon, Elder Moon (11/25–12/22), Groundhog Mother's Moon, Moon before Yule, Moon of Long Nights or Long Night or Long Night's Moon, Moon of Popping Trees, Moon of Vision, Peach Moon, Rowan Moon, Snow Moon, Spirit Moon, Twelfth Moon, and Wolf Moon.

It is a powerful time for banishing, divination, pathworking, astral projection, male magick, positive magick, vision quests, and for workings that are related to empowerment, endurance, healing, prosperity, transformation, wholeness, wisdom, and interpersonal connections. It is also an auspicious time for workings to free yourself from the control of others.

✑ Disseminating Moon
(the third to seventh days after the Full Moon)

The Disseminating Moon is a powerful time for banishing, meditation (especially on your accomplishments), and workings that are related to addictions, creativity, decisions, decline, decrease, divorce, emotions, health, protection, sharing, and stress. It is also an auspicious time for workings to end strife.

Disseminating Moon Correspondences
See Waning Moon

Waning Moon

(also called Third Quarter Moon; the seventh to tenth days after the Full Moon)

Widdershins go when the Moon doth wane,
An' the Werewolf howls by the dread Wolfsbane.
—REDE OF THE WICCAE

The Waning Moon is a powerful time for averting, banishing, binding, clearing, divination, releasing, Crone magick, and workings that are related to balance, change, conclusion, darkness, death, decisions, decrease, divorce, endings, evaluation, intuition, justice, prophecy, protection, quarrels, rebirth, rejection, release, removal, resolution, reversal, reworking, self-criticism, separation, spirituality, transformation, weakness, wisdom, Crone power, deep secrets, inner secrets, old age, simple life, the Underworld, and death and resurrection.

In the body, this is an appropriate time for workings that are related to disease, menopause, chronic illness, loss of consciousness, and the power of healing. It is also a good time for workings to banish addictions, diminish aches and pains, and reduce obesity or high cholesterol. With respect to people, it's a great time for workings that are related to Crones, enemies, divorced people, the elderly, and post-menopausal women.

The Waning Moon is also an auspicious time to conjure spirits, purify an athame, and to banish, end, diminish, overcome, reduce, release, remove, stop, and winnow. Rid yourself of all that is baneful to you during the Waning Moon, such as in workings to overcome diseases, remove hexes, reverse fortune, stop losses, banish negative influences, winnow negative people, end problems or bad habits, and release negative attachments or situations.

Waning Moon Correspondences

Waning Moon/West/Predawn Hours/Autumn/Winter

Color: black, gray, purple

Animal: oyster, werewolf

Plant: wolfbane ☠

Goddess: Annis (Black Annis), Ashi Vanguhi, Astarte, Atropos, Bendis, Cailleach, the Crone, Ereshkigal, Hecate, Ialysa, Inanna, the Kali Nityas, Levanah (Lunar Flame), Lilith, Nephthys

God: Tammuz

Evocation: Benthesicyme, Chrysothemis, the Hesperides (Westerly Ones), night spirits

✤ Waning Crescent Moon

(the tenth day after the Full Moon until the Moon is no longer visible)

The horns of the Moon face right during the Waning Crescent Moon. It is a powerful time for banishing, clearing, meditation, inner work, and for workings that are related to decrease, diminishment, ebb, reduction, and understanding. Examples include workings to break habits or lose weight. Hair cut at this time will grow back slowly.

Waning Crescent Moon Correspondences
Waning Crescent/Night

Color: black, gray

Goddess: Hecate, Sesheta

✧ Dark Moon

(also called Black Moon and Lost Moon; the three days when the Moon cannot be seen, eleven to fourteen days after the Full Moon)

Some practitioners say that no magick should be performed at this time because of unpredictable results. They use Dark Moon energy for divination, deep meditation, dream work, vision quests, or to rest and recharge. Others consider the Dark Moon a powerful time for banishing, clearing, Crone magick, inner work, and for workings that are related to addiction(s), answers, change, darkness, death, doubt, endings, enemies, healing, illumination, intuition, invisibility, justice, loneliness, obstacles, quarrels, questions, separation, solitude, wisdom, inner strength, old age, personal matters, spiritual understanding, and the Mysteries. They also see it as an auspicious time for workings to battle attackers, impose justice, reject negativity, deal with anger, and understand your dark side.

Workings must be completed before the Dark Moon reaches its darkest point. It then becomes the New Moon, which has very different energies.

Dark Moon Correspondences (see also, Black Moon)

Dark Moon/Morning/Winter

Color: black

Goddess: the Crone, Hecate (Goddess of the Dark of the Moon), Lilith

✧ Void of Course Moon

(when it does not make aspects to planets)

The Void of Course Moon occurs every several days, and can last minutes, hours, or days. It fluctuates widely and ends when the Moon enters an astrological house, so an annual astrological almanac is needed to track it. This is a time that, in a sense, is *not* time, because the Moon is between realms. It is powerful for confusion, detachment, disconnection, fallibility, inconstancy, miscommunication, bad decisions, false starts, unexpected results, wasted efforts, and wrong answers. Some practitioners hold that you can overcome it by doubling magickal energy, but spells cast at this time will generally not manifest, and anything begun during this time will usually not succeed.

The Void of Course Moon is, instead, an auspicious time for meditation, astral projection, and inner work. It is also a good time to rest and recharge magickal batteries. The exception, say some, is when the Moon is void of course in the houses of Cancer, Pisces, Sagittarius, or Taurus. They consider that a powerful time for workings that correspond to those signs (see Astrological Year).

Blue Moon

**(also called Goal Moon and Hearth Moon;
when a Full Moon appears twice in the same
calendar month; or the third of four Full Moons
occurring in the same quarter of a year)**

A Blue Moon is a powerful time for divination, wish magick, and workings that are related to fertility, goals, love, prophecy, protection, the home, and the rare and unusual. It is also an auspicious time for workings to learn lessons, manifest truth, and improve your life. The moonlight of a Blue Moon is considered especially potent, and thought to have the power to speak to anything upon which it shines.

Blue Moon Correspondences

Color: blue (every shade)

Sidhe Moon

(also called Fairy Moon, Moon of the Other People, Black Moon, and Other Moon; the second New Moon occurring in one calendar month)

A Sidhe Moon is a powerful time for fairy magick and workings that are related to productivity, creative expression, fairy power, and the Other-world. It is also an auspicious time to find an animal or spirit guide.

Sidhe Moon Correspondences (see also Black Moon)

Animal: familiars

Plant: white flowers

Evocation: fairies

Dry Moon

(also called Cheshire Moon)

A Dry Moon can be seen in the northern hemisphere during Summer, when the horns of a Crescent Moon appear to tilt, so that the Moon looks like a vessel that could hold any liquid poured into it. In Hawaiian mythology, this was an explanation for dry weather.

A Dry Moon is an auspicious time for workings to hold on to things, such as money, possessions, or relationships.

Wet Moon

(also called Dripping Wet Moon)

A Wet Moon can be seen in the northern hemisphere during Winter, when the horns of the Crescent Moon appear to tilt, so that the Moon looks like a vessel that would spill any liquid poured into it. In Hawaiian mythology, this was an explanation for rain.

A Wet Moon is an auspicious time for releasing and for workings that are related to abundance, fertility, and rain.

Wet Moon Correspondences

Water

God: Kaelo (Water Bearer)

⚬ **Black Moon**

This term can be confusing because it has five meanings, in different traditions.

1. A second New Moon occurring in one calendar month.

2. The third of four New Moons occurring in one quarter of a year.

3. A time before the New Moon when the Moon cannot easily be seen with the naked eye.

4. A calendar month without a Full Moon. This usually happens in a February.

5. A calendar month without a New Moon or a Dark Moon. This usually happens in a February.

Black Moon Correspondences (see Dark Moon)

Daily Solar Cycles

Dawn and twilight are both potent with magickal energy because each is a time-between-time, neither light nor dark. Noon is the time of maximum solar energy. Midnight is the traditional "witching hour"—a time-between-time as one day becomes another. Some ancient Egyptian magickal texts called for workings to be repeated four times on the same day, at sunrise, noon, sunset, and midnight. That is something that you may wish to incorporate into your practice for major undertakings.

❧ Sunrise

Dawn, like the Waxing Year and the New Moon, is a powerful time for deosil magick: constructive workings that attract, charge, improve, increase, invite, strengthen, and overcome. Like the New Moon, it is an auspicious time for workings that are related to beginnings, birth, growth, initiation, optimism, raising, rebirth, rejuvenation, renewal, cyclical rebeginning, erotic dreams, fresh starts, new ideas, new partnerships, new projects, new relationships, and new ventures. It is also a great time for chanting, meditation, releasing, visualization, Air magick/rituals/spells, and for workings that are related to ascent, awakening, crossroads, emergence, employment, healing, health, hope, light, love, modesty, opening, possibilities, purification, resurrection, return, romance, self-improvement, study, youth, auspicious beginnings, business success, morning light, nourishing dew, and the conscious mind.

Sunrise is also an appropriate time to begin spells, make offerings, say affirmations, gather magickal plants, kindle sacred fire, invoke or worship dawn deities, dispose of used liquid spell ingredients (by tossing them outdoors toward the East), and for workings to break addictions, banish or overcome darkness, perform satires over rulers, make solar charms and recipes, see that promises are kept, activate the potential of a new day, and get a new angle on a problem. A naked priestess can bless a field by circling it deosil at dawn.

Sunrise Correspondences

Sun/Rising Sun/Air/East/Male/Dawn/Spring

Color: gold, orange, peach, pink, rose

Charm: Orphic Cup (goat's milk with honey), scarab

Animal: baboon, white horse, platypus, rooster, all birds that sing near dawn, and all creatures that are active at sunrise

Plant: daffodil, ladies mantle (use dew found on the leaves at dawn as a charm for female problems), vervain, and all plants with flowers that open near sunrise

Goddess: Aja, Albina, Amaterasu (Great Shining Heaven), Atanea, Aurora (Golden Dawn, Herald of the Sun), Auska, Austrine, Aya, Bast (Lady of the East), Bezla, Chasca, Chun T'i, Dilbah (She Who Opens the Heavens in Her Supremacy), Eos (Dawn Maiden, She of the East), Etain, Gendenwitha, Hanwi, Hathor, Iris, Ishtar (Queen of the Rising of the Sun), Isis (Maker of the Sunrise, Mistress of the Dawn, Goddess of the Rosy Dawn), the Maiden, Marici, Mater Matuta, Ostara (Rising Light, Radiant Dawn), Rohini (Red One), Sengen-Sama, Tefnut (Dew of Dawn), Theia, Thesan, Ushas, Waka-Hiru-Me, Xoli-Kaltes, Yolkai Estsan (White Shell Woman), Dawn Zorya

God: Amon, Aruna, Auilix, Cautes, Dellingr, Enlil (Lord of Air), Harmakhis (Horus in the Horizon), Heimdall, Horus, Janus, Kephera (He Who Has Come Forth), Ku, Lucifer (Light-Bringer, Son of Morning), Mithras (Rising Sun), Nefertem, Ptah (Opener), Salim, Savitar, Shahar, Tlahuizcalpantecuhtli (Lord of the House of Dawn), Tlalchitonatiuh, Vohu Manah

Evocation: Bean Nighe, Gazardiel, Michael

🌿 Noon

As Full Moon is the time of maximum lunar power, noon is the time of maximum solar power. It is a great time for centering, solar magick, Fire magick/rituals/spells, and workings that are related to courage, energy, money, protection, and strength. It is also an auspicious time for all workings of the Sun, such as the making of solar charms and recipes.

Noon Correspondences

Sun/Fire/Center/Noon/Summer/Leo

Color: yellow, white

Goddess: Hemera (Queen of Day), the Mother

God: Mithras, Ra (Lord of Rays)

🌿 Sunset

Like the Waning Year and the Waning Moon, dusk is a power time for widdershins magick: workings that avert, banish, clear, decrease, end, lessen, repel, or weaken. Twilight is also a great time for meditation, prayer, visualization, mirror magick, Water magick/rituals/spells, and workings that are related to closure, conclusion, darkness, death, endings, hopelessness, removal, resolution, reversal, sorrow, transformation, and weight loss.

Sunset Correspondences

Sun/Setting Sun/Water/West/Female/Dusk/Autumn/Winter

Color: blue, indigo, orange, pink, purple, red

Stone: amethyst

Animal: fox, lion, owl, platypus, all creatures that become active at dusk

Plant: all night-blooming plants and trees

Goddess: Annis, Atargatis, Bast, Breksta, the Crone, the Dark Goddess, Dysis, Hanwi, Nephthys, Sandhya, Sekhmet (Lady of the West, Mistress of the Evening Barque), Dusk Zorya

God: Amon (The Hidden One), Astraios, Atum (The Closer), Baal, Baal Qarnaim (Two-Horned Ba'al), Cautopates, Janus, Mithras, Osiris, Savitar, Set, Shalim, Tayau Sakaimoka

Evocation: Bean Nighe, Endymion, the Hesperides (the Westerly Ones, Daughters of the West)

❦ Midnight

Midnight, the traditional witching hour, is prime time for magick. It is auspicious for any working, but specific for candle magick, sex magick, Earth magick/rituals/spells, and for workings that are related to crossroads and truth.

Midnight Correspondences
Venus/Full Moon/Earth/North/Taurus

Color: black, midnight blue, dark green

Animal: bat, owl, toad

Goddess: Aeval, Hecate (Dark Mother, Goddess of Midnight), Midnight Zorya

God: Baal Zephon (Lord of the North)

✒ Night Sun

It is easy to forget that the Sun is still there at night—still powerfully impacting the Earth and still available for magick. Night is a power time for solar workings that are related to cloaking, invisibility, underestimation, hidden power, and surreptitious advantage.

Night Sun Correspondences
Sun/Night

Color: black, clear

Animal: all nocturnal creatures

Plant: all night-blooming plants and trees

Goddess: Midnight Zorya

God: Amon (The Hidden One), Atum, Seker (He Who Is Shut In)

Annual Solar Cycles

See Waxing Year/Waning Year
See Astrological Year

PART FOUR

Intent and the
Wheels of the Year

SE THIS SECTION of this book to determine the most auspicious times for your workings.

Abundance

Sunday/first hour after sunrise on Thursday/first hour after sunset on Sunday/Waxing Moon/Wet Moon/Autumn/Taurus

to attract abundance: Taurus

Astral Projection

Monday/first hour after sunrise on Monday/first hour after sunset on Thursday/Full Moon in February or December/Void of Course Moon

astral work: first hour after sunrise on Saturday/first hour after sunset on Tuesday

Attraction

Waxing Year/Waxing Moon/Full Moon/Dawn/first hour after sunrise on Sunday or Friday/first hour after sunset on Monday or Wednesday/Sunday/May/Libra *to attract abundance:* Taurus

to attract affection: first hour after sunrise on Friday/first hour after sunset on Monday

to attract attention: Sunday

to attract blessings: first hour after sunrise on Sunday/first hour after sunset on Wednesday

to attract the Goddess: first hour after sunrise on Monday/first hour after sunset on Thursday

to attract gods: first hour after sunrise on Sunday/first hour after sunset on Wednesday

to attract good luck: Waxing Moon

to attract honors: first hour after sunrise on Sunday/first hour after sunset on Wednesday

to attract love: Waxing Year/New Moon/first hour after sunrise on Friday/first hour after sunset on Monday

to attract love from women: Thursday

to attract luck: Friday

to attract lust: first hour after sunrise on Friday/first hour after sunset on Monday

to attract money: Full Moon/first hour after sunrise on Sunday/first hour after sunset on Wednesday/Friday

to attract prosperity: first hour after sunrise on Thursday or Friday/first hour after sunset on Sunday or Monday

to attract whatever you need: wash your doorstep with inward motions at dawn on a Wednesday

to attract yang: first hour after sunrise on Sunday/first hour after sunset on Wednesday

to attract yin: first hour after sunrise on Monday/first hour after sunset on Thursday

to attract more of what you already have: Thursday

Averting

Waning Year/Waning Moon/Sunset/Saturday

to avert darkness: first hour after sunrise on Sunday/first hour after sunset on Wednesday

to avert doubt(s): Monday

to avert evil: Waning Year/Friday/Saturday

to avert fear(s): Monday

to avert negative energy: June

to avert negativity: Saturday

Awakening

Dawn/first hour after sunrise on Sunday/first hour after sunset on Wednesday/Spring/April/Full Moon in April

spiritual awakening: Aries

to awaken anything that has been dormant: Spring

to awaken fertility: Spring

to awaken understanding: first hour after sunrise on Sunday/first hour after sunset on Wednesday

Balance

Friday/first hour after sunrise on Monday/first hour after sunset on Thursday/Waning Moon/Full Moon in March, May, or September/June/October/November/Gemini/Cancer/Libra/Spring Equinox/Autumn Equinox

emotional balance: Libra

karmic balance: Libra

spiritual balance: Libra

to balance inconsistencies: June

to balance light and darkness: March

to balance positive and negative forces: Libra

Banishing

Sunset/Saturday/first hour after sunrise on Tuesday or Saturday/first hour after sunset on Tuesday or Friday/Waning Year/Waning Moon/Waning Crescent Moon/Dark Moon/Full Moon in February, September, October, November, or December/Disseminating Moon/Winter/January

to banish addictions: Waning Moon

to banish anxiety: first hour after sunrise on Thursday/first hour after sunset on Sunday

to banish bad habits: Waning Year

to banish darkness: Dawn/first hour after sunrise on Sunday/first hour after sunset on Wednesday *to banish depression:* Thursday

to banish evil: Sunday

to banish harm: first hour after sunrise on Saturday/first hour after sunset on Tuesday

to banish negative forces: Saturday

to banish negative influences: Saturday/Waning Moon

to banish negative thoughts: Full Moon in November

to banish negativity: Tuesday/Thursday/first hour after sunrise on Sunday/first hour after sunset on Wednesday

to banish negativity of the previous calendar year: January

to banish Winter: February

Battle

Tuesday/first hour after sunrise on Tuesday/first hour after sunset on Friday/Autumn/Aries

battlefield magick: first hour after sunrise on Tuesday/first hour after sunset on Friday

battlefields: Tuesday

to battle attackers: Dark Moon

Beginning (s)

Dawn/Tuesday/first hour after sunrise on Tuesday/first hour after sunset on Friday/New Moon/Waxing Moon/Waxing

Crescent Moon/Full Moon in January or November/Spring/ January/March/Aries

auspicious beginning(s): Dawn/first hour after sunrise on Friday or Sunday/first hour after sunset on Monday or Wednesday

cyclical rebeginning: Dawn/New Moon/Spring

new beginnings: Tuesday/Waxing Moon/Full Moon in March/April

rebeginning: Sunrise/Spring

to begin anything new: first hour after sunrise on Monday/first hour after sunset on Thursday/New Moon

to begin any magickal operation: Sunday

to begin projects: March

to begin a spell: Dawn/Waxing Moon

to begin workings that will take a long time to complete: New Moon

Binding

Saturday/first hour after sunrise on Saturday/first hour after sunset on Tuesday/Waning Moon/Full Moon in May, June, July, or October

to bind negative forces: Saturday/first hour after sunrise on Saturday/first hour after sunset on Tuesday

to bind negative influences: Saturday

to bind spirits: Wednesday

Blessings

July/Full Moon in July

solar blessings: first hour after sunrise on Sunday/first hour after sunset on Wednesday

to attract blessings: first hour after sunrise on Sunday/first hour after sunset on Wednesday

to bless a field: Dawn, blessed by a naked priestess circling it deosil

to count your blessings: August

to receive blessings: first hour after sunrise on Saturday/first hour after sunset on Tuesday

Business

Sunday/Tuesday/Wednesday/Thursday/first hour after sunrise on Wednesday, Thursday, Friday, or Saturday/first hour after sunset on Saturday, Sunday, Monday, or Tuesday/Waxing Crescent Moon/Capricorn

business ethics: first hour after sunrise on Sunday/first hour after sunset on Wednesday

businesspeople: (see People)

business success: Dawn/Virgo

business transactions: first hour after sunrise on Wednesday/first hour after sunset on Saturday

business travel: Sagittarius

to expand a business: Sagittarius

to grow a business: first hour after sunrise on Thursday/first hour after sunset on Sunday

to increase business: Thursday

Career

Sunday/Saturday/first hour after sunrise on Sunday/first hour after sunset on Wednesday/New Moon/Leo/Capricorn

career goals: Sunday

Centering

Noon/Thursday/first hour after sunrise on Saturday/first hour after sunset on Tuesday

Change(s)

Sunday/Monday/Friday/Saturday/first hour after sunrise on Monday or Wednesday/first hour after sunset on Thursday or Saturday/Waning Moon/Dark Moon/Full Moon (especially in April or October)/Waxing Crescent Moon/March/April/June/September/December/Gemini/Scorpio

changeability: first hour after sunrise on Monday/first hour after sunset on Thursday/Gemini

positive change: Waxing Moon/Sagittarius

sudden changes: Aquarius

to activate change: Sunday/first hour after sunrise on Sunday/first hour after sunset on Wednesday *to make changes:* Gemini

willingness to change: first hour after sunrise on Monday/first hour after sunset on Thursday

Charging

Dawn/Waxing Year/Waxing Moon

to charge magickal tools: Waxing Year

to charge talismans: Waxing Moon

Clarity

Full Moon

clarity leading to wisdom: New Moon

clear mind/mental clarity: Wednesday/first hour after sunrise on Monday/first hour after sunset on Thursday

Clearing

Sunset/Waning Year/Waning Moon/Waning Crescent Moon/ Dark Moon/February/September/Full Moon in February or September

to clear backlogs and blockages that prevent progress: September

to clear entities: Waning Year

to clear negative vibrations: Full Moon in November

to clear negativity: July

to rid yourself of all that is baneful to you: Waning Moon

Communication(s)

Wednesday/first hour after sunrise on Wednesday/first hour after sunset on Saturday/June/Gemini

communicators: (see People)

correspondence: first hour after sunrise on Wednesday/first hour after sunset on Saturday

honest communication: Sagittarius

messages: Wednesday/first hour after sunrise on Wednesday/first hour after sunset on Saturday

messenger services: first hour after sunrise on Monday/first hour after sunset on Thursday

messengers: first hour after sunrise on Monday/first hour after sunset on Thursday

miscommunication: Void of Course Moon

psychic messages: Capricorn

spirit communication: Saturday/November/Full Moon in October/Pisces

to send mail: Gemini/Virgo/Sagittarius/Pisces

to send over long distances: Capricorn

written communication: Wednesday

Confidence

Sunday/first hour after sunrise on Sunday/first hour after sunset on Wednesday/January/Aries/Leo/Sagittarius/Capricorn *self-confidence:* Sunday/first hour after sunrise on Sunday/first hour after sunset on Wednesday/April/Full Moon in April/Sagittarius

Courage

Noon/Tuesday/Friday/first hour after sunrise on Sunday or Tuesday/first hour after sunset on Wednesday or Friday/Waxing Moon/Summer/March/August/November/Full Moon in July or October/Aries/Leo/Sagittarius

Death

Sunset/Tuesday/first hour after sunrise on Saturday/first hour after sunset on Tuesday/Waning Moon/Dark Moon/Autumn/Winter/Scorpio/Capricorn/Pisces

death and resurrection: Waning Moon

to overcome death: first hour after sunrise on Sunday/first hour after sunset on Wednesday

to release the dead: Saturday

violent death: first hour after sunrise on Tuesday/first hour after sunset on Friday

Decisions

Thursday/Full Moon/Disseminating Moon/Waning Moon

bad decisions: Void of Course Moon

decisiveness: Aries

to make decisions: June

Defense

Sunday/Saturday/first hour after sunrise on Saturday, Sunday or Tuesday/first hour after sunset on Tuesday, Wednesday, or Friday/Full Moon in April

psychic defense: first hour after sunrise on Saturday/first hour after sunset on Tuesday

psychic self-defense: Saturday

Discovery

Saturday/first hour after sunrise on Wednesday/first hour after sunset on Saturday/May

to discover secrets: Monday

Divination

Sunday/Monday/first hour after sunrise on Sunday, Monday, or Wednesday/first hour after sunset on Wednesday, Thursday, or Saturday/Full Moon (especially in February, July, August, or December)/Waning Moon/Dark Moon/Blue Moon/January/ July/Cancer/Scorpio/Pisces

divination tools: first hour after sunrise on Monday/first hour after sunset on Thursday

runes: Wednesday

scrying: Autumn/Full Moon

to learn a new method of divination: October

weather divination: January

Dreams

Monday/first hour after sunrise on Monday/first hour after sunset on Thursday/Full Moon/Winter

erotic dreams: Dawn/New Moon

lucid dreaming: Monday

prophetic dreams: first hour after sunrise on Monday/first hour after sunset on Thursday/Full Moon

psychic dreams: first hour after sunrise on Monday/first hour after sunset on Thursday/Pisces

Dream Work

Monday/Friday/first hour after sunrise on Monday/first hour after sunset on Thursday/Dark Moon/Full Moon (especially in May or July)/Winter/July/Aquarius/Pisces

dream magick: Friday/Winter

Education

Tuesday/Wednesday/first hour after sunrise on Thursday/first hour after sunset on Sunday/Virgo/Sagittarius

educators: Wednesday/Sagittarius

higher education: Wednesday/Thursday/first hour after sunrise on Thursday/first hour after sunset on Sunday

Employment

Dawn/Sunday/Thursday/Autumn/Virgo

employers: Sunday/Thursday

jobs: Aries/Virgo

to find a job: New Moon/Full Moon

to hire employees: Wednesday

Ending(s)

Sunset/Waning Year/Saturday/first hour after sunrise on Saturday/first hour after sunset on Tuesday/Waning Moon/Dark Moon/Winter/Pisces

to end bad habits: first hour after sunrise on Saturday/first hour after sunset on Tuesday/Waning Moon/Aquarius

to end connections: Scorpio

to end enmity: Sunday/first hour after sunrise on Sunday/first hour after sunset on Wednesday

to end illness: Waning Year

to end legal matters: first hour after sunrise on Sunday/first hour after sunset on Wednesday

to end problems: Waning Moon

to end quarrels: Thursday

to end strife: first hour after sunrise on Saturday/first hour after sunset on Tuesday/New Moon/Disseminating Moon

to see things through to their ends: Full Moon

Energy

Noon/Tuesday/first hour after sunrise on Sunday or Tuesday/first hour after sunset on Wednesday or Friday/Full Moon/March/Aries/Sagittarius

bioenergy: Sunday/first hour after sunrise on Sunday/first hour after sunset on Wednesday

creative energy: Waxing Moon/May/Aries/Leo/Sagittarius

divine energy: first hour after sunrise on Sunday/first hour after sunset on Wednesday

healing energy: first hour after sunrise on Sunday/first hour after sunset on Wednesday

physical energy: Sunday/first hour after sunrise on Sunday or Tuesday/first hour after sunset on Wednesday or Friday/Tuesday

positive energy: first hour after sunrise on Sunday/first hour after sunset on Wednesday

power of positive energy to overcome negative energy: February

projective energy: first hour after sunrise on Sunday or Tuesday/first hour after sunset on Wednesday or Friday/Aries/Leo/Sagittarius

psychic energy: Full Moon/Cancer/Scorpio/Pisces

receptive energy: first hour after sunrise on Monday or Friday/first hour after sunset on Monday or Thursday/Taurus/Cancer/Virgo/Scorpio/Capricorn/Pisces

solar energy: Noon/first hour after sunrise on Sunday/first hour after sunset on Wednesday *to avert negative energy:* June *to boost ritual energy:* Sunday/first hour after sunrise on Sunday/first hour after sunset on Wednesday

to boost sexual energy: first hour after sunrise on Sunday, Tuesday, or Friday/first hour after sunset on Monday, Wednesday, or Friday/Scorpio

to channel healing energy: Scorpio

to channel magickal energy: Dawn/Sunset/Sunday/first hour after sunrise on Sunday/first hour after sunset on Wednesday/Full Moon/Summer

to energize chakras: first hour after sunrise on Sunday/first hour after sunset on Wednesday

to energize spells: first hour after sunrise on Friday/first hour after sunset on Monday

to overcome negative energy: February

to replenish energy: July

to send energy: first hour after sunrise on Monday/first hour after sunset on Thursday

to use energy to fight: first hour after sunrise on Monday/first hour after sunset on Thursday

Trickster energy: first hour after sunrise on Wednesday/first hour after sunset on Saturday

Exploration

March/May/Full Moon in March/Aries/Sagittarius

explorers: Aries/Sagittarius

Family

Saturday/first hour after sunrise on Monday/first hour after sunset on Thursday/Full Moon in November/Cancer

family life: Cancer

family matters: Full Moon in October

family members: (see People)

family ties: June

Favor(s)

Sunday/first hour after sunrise on Sunday or Thursday/first hour after sunset on Sunday or Wednesday/Virgo/Libra/Capricorn

to get favors: Sunday

Fertility

Monday/Friday/first hour after sunrise on Sunday, Monday, or Friday/first hour after sunset on Monday, Wednesday, or Thursday/Waxing Moon/Full Moon (especially in March, April, May, June, July, August, September, October, or November)/Blue Moon/Wet Moon/Spring/February/April/May/Cancer/Leo/Scorpio *female fertility:* Monday/first hour after sunrise on Monday/first hour after sunset on Thursday

fertility of land, Nature, plants: first hour after sunrise on Sunday/first hour after sunset on Wednesday

infertility: Gemini/Leo/Virgo

male fertility: Tuesday/Thursday

to activate fertility: first hour after sunrise on Sunday or Monday/first hour after sunset on Wednesday or Thursday

to awaken fertility: Spring

Fidelity

Thursday/Full Moon in June/August

Financial Matters (see also Money)

Sunday/Thursday/Saturday/first hour after sunrise on Wednesday or Friday/first hour after sunset on Saturday or Monday

financial gain: Sunday/first hour after sunrise on Sunday/first hour after sunset on Wednesday

financial planners: Virgo

financial security: Capricorn

financial speculation: first hour after sunrise on Thursday/first hour after sunset on Sunday

new financial projects: Aries

personal finances: Sunday/first hour after sunrise on Friday/first hour after sunset on Monday

shared finances: Saturday

to lessen financial problems: Waning Year

Friendship

Sunday/Monday/Friday/first hour after sunrise on Sunday or Friday/first hour after sunset on Monday or Wednesday/ Waxing Moon/Full Moon in August/Summer/June/August/Leo/ Aquarius

friendliness: Sagittarius/Aquarius

friends: (see People)

new friendships: New Moon

to encourage friendships: first hour after sunrise on Thursday/first hour after sunset on Sunday

universal friendship: Aquarius

Goals

Sunday/first hour after sunrise on Sunday or Tuesday/first hour after sunset on Wednesday or Friday/Waxing Crescent Moon/ January/Full Moon in May/Blue Moon/Capricorn

career goals: Sunday

male goals: Tuesday

spiritual goals: July/Full Moon in July

to achieve/attain goals: Sunday/first hour after sunrise on Saturday/first hour after sunset on Tuesday/Full Moon

to work on/toward goals: Gibbous Moon/January

Grounding

First hour after sunrise on Tuesday or Saturday/first hour after sunset on Friday or Tuesday/Winter

Growth

Dawn/Sunday/Thursday/Friday/first hour after sunrise on Sunday, Monday, Tuesday, or Thursday/first hour after sunset on Wednesday, Thursday, Friday, or Sunday/Waxing Moon/New Moon/ Gibbous Moon/Full Moon (especially in February or April)/Spring/February/March/April/May/Aries/Cancer/Leo/Scorpio

evolutionary growth: Aquarius

new growth: Spring

personal growth: New Moon

psychic growth: Scorpio

rapid growth: first hour after sunrise on Sunday/first hour after sunset on Wednesday

spiritual growth: Monday/first hour after sunrise on Monday/first hour after sunset on Thursday/September

to discourage growth of hair: cut it during the Waning Crescent Moon

to encourage growth of hair: cut it at Full Moon

to grow a business: first hour after sunrise on Thursday/first hour after sunset on Sunday

to grow strong: June

to help a garden grow: first hour after sunrise on Sunday/first hour after sunset on Wednesday

Happiness

Sunday/first hour after sunrise on Sunday or Friday/first hour after sunset on Wednesday or Monday/May/Full Moon in May

contentment: July

male happiness: Thursday

Healing

Dawn/Sunday/Monday/Tuesday/Wednesday/Thursday/Friday/first hour after sunrise on Sunday, Monday, Wednesday, or Friday/first hour after sunset on Monday, Wednesday, Thursday, or Saturday/New Moon/Waxing Moon/Full Moon (especially in February, March, May, August, September, October, November, or December)/Dark Moon/Spring/January/February/June/Gemini/Virgo/Scorpio/Aquarius

emotional healing: Monday

healing energy: first hour after sunrise on Sunday/first hour after sunset on Wednesday

healing power: first hour after sunrise on Sunday/first hour after sunset on Wednesday/Waxing Moon/Scorpio

177

healing touch: Scorpio

physical healing: Friday/Saturday

power of healing: Waning Moon

sexual healing: first hour after sunrise on Friday/first hour after sunset on Monday

to channel healing energy: Scorpio

to get in touch with the universal healing force: Aquarius

to heal after surgery: first hour after sunrise on Tuesday/first hour after sunset on Friday

to heal serious illness: Full Moon

to heal with light: first hour after sunrise on Sunday/first hour after sunset on Wednesday

to heal wounds: Monday

to speed healing: first hour after sunrise on Wednesday/first hour after sunset on Saturday

Home

Monday/first hour after sunrise on Monday/first hour after sunset on Thursday/Blue Moon/Taurus/Cancer

home improvements: Friday

to buy a home: Taurus/Leo/Scorpio/Aquarius

to move house: Taurus/Aquarius

to protect the home: Full Moon in October

Honesty

October/Taurus/Sagittarius

honest communication: Sagittarius

to be honest with yourself: January

Increase

Dawn/Thursday/first hour after sunrise on Monday or Thursday/first hour after sunset on Thursday or Sunday/Waxing Year/New Moon/Waxing Moon/Waxing Crescent Moon/Gibbous Moon/Full Moon/Spring/Leo

psychic increase: Waxing Moon

to increase business: Thursday

to increase income: Waxing Year

to increase money: Waxing Moon

to increase psychic abilities: first hour after sunrise on Monday/first hour after sunset on Thursday/Full Moon

to increase psychic awareness: first hour after sunrise on Saturday/first hour after sunset on Tuesday

to increase ritual energy: first hour after sunrise on Sunday/first hour after sunset on Wednesday

to increase status: Capricorn

Initiation

Dawn/Monday/New Moon/February

initiation into the mysteries of love: first hour after sunrise on Friday/first hour after sunset on Monday

occult initiation: Scorpio

Inner Work

Sunday/first hour after sunrise on Monday/first hour after sunset on Thursday/Waning Crescent Moon/Dark Moon/ Void of Course Moon/Autumn/Winter/January/September/ December/Full Moon in June or November

inner beauty: Friday

inner child: Leo

inner depths: Scorpio

inner eye of wisdom: first hour after sunrise on Monday/first hour after sunset on Thursday

inner harmony: October/Full Moon in October

inner knowledge: Full Moon

inner peace: Taurus

inner power: Scorpio

inner secrets: Waning Moon

inner strength: Dark Moon

inner vision: February/May

inner wisdom: first hour after sunrise on Monday/first hour after sunset on Thursday/Full Moon

self-awareness: Aries/Libra/Scorpio

self-confidence: (see Confidence)

self-control: Aries/Full Moon in June

self-criticism: Waning Moon/Virgo

self-destruction: Scorpio

self-discipline: Thursday/Saturday/Capricorn

self-esteem: Thursday/Saturday/Aries

self-examination: Libra

self-expression: Wednesday/Gemini

self-guidance: Full Moon in February or April

self-image: Libra

self-improvement: Dawn/Wednesday/Thursday/first hour after sunrise on Wednesday/first hour after sunset on Saturday/New Moon/Full Moon

self-knowledge: Sunday/Full Moon

self-promotion: Leo

self-reinforcement: first hour after sunrise on Thursday/first hour after sunset on Sunday

self-reliance: April/Full Moon in April

self-renewal: first hour after sunrise on Monday/first hour after sunset on Thursday

self-respect: Full Moon in February or April/Leo

self-sacrifice: Sagittarius

self-sufficiency: Capricorn

self-worth: Thursday

spiritual self: Pisces

to appreciate yourself: Virgo

to assert yourself: Tuesday/first hour after sunrise on Tuesday/first hour after sunset on Friday

to be honest with yourself: January

to dedicate yourself: February

to free yourself from the control of others: Full Moon in December

to let yourself shine: December

to push yourself: Capricorn

to test yourself: April

to understand yourself: October

Inspiration

First hour after sunrise on Monday or Wednesday/first hour after sunset on Thursday or Saturday/Waxing Moon (strongest when the Moon is nearly Full)/Full Moon (especially in August or October)/February/May/Pisces

mystical inspiration: Pisces

spiritual inspiration: Pisces

to inspire others: Leo

Inviting

Dawn/Waxing Year/Waxing Moon

to invite love: Waxing Moon

to invite success: Waxing Year

Justice

Monday/Thursday/Saturday/first hour after sunrise on Sunday, Thursday, or Saturday/first hour after sunset on Sunday, Tuesday, or Wednesday/Waning Moon/Dark Moon/Full Moon in October/October/Libra/Pisces

to bring someone to justice: Saturday/first hour after sunrise on Saturday/first hour after sunset on Tuesday

to impose justice: Dark Moon

Knowledge

Wednesday/first hour after sunrise on Saturday/first hour after sunset on Tuesday/Saturday/Waxing Moon/Full Moon/Aquarius

inner knowledge: Full Moon

instinctual knowledge: Cancer

magickal knowledge: first hour after sunrise on Saturday/first hour after sunset on Tuesday

omnipresent knowledge: first hour after sunrise on Sunday/first hour after sunset on Wednesday *sacred knowledge:* Full Moon

self-knowledge: Sunday/Full Moon

spiritual knowledge: Full Moon in March

to share knowledge: Full Moon

Learning

Sunday/Wednesday/first hour after sunrise on Wednesday/first hour after sunset on Saturday/Sagittarius

higher learning: Tuesday

to learn lessons: Blue Moon

to learn a new method of divination: October

Legal Matters (see also Justice)

Sunday/Thursday/first hour after sunrise on Sunday/first hour after sunset on Wednesday/Full Moon/Libra/Sagittarius

court cases: Thursday/Sagittarius

courtrooms: Tuesday

courts: Sunday

judges: (see People)

karmic law: Saturday

law(s): Sunday/Wednesday/Thursday/Saturday/first hour after sunrise on Sunday or Thursday/first hour after sunset on Wednesday or Sunday/December/Sagittarius *law enforcement:* first hour after sunrise on Tuesday/first hour after sunset on Friday/Libra

law enforcers: (see People)

lawsuits: Tuesday

lawyers: Tuesday/Libra

legality: Tuesday

legal problems: first hour after sunrise on Thursday/first hour after sunset on Sunday

metaphysical laws: Sagittarius

to end legal matters: first hour after sunrise on Sunday/first hour after sunset on Wednesday

to settle legal matters: first hour after sunrise on Thursday/first hour after sunset on Sunday

Life

Saturday/first hour after sunrise on Sunday/first hour after sunset on Wednesday

the cycle of life: first hour after sunrise on Monday/first hour after sunset on Thursday

eternal life: Aquarius

family life: Cancer

the life force: first hour after sunrise on Sunday/first hour after sunset on Wednesday/Spring

new life: April

religious life: Sagittarius

simple life: Waning Moon

to calm down your life: first hour after sunrise on Monday/first hour after sunset on Thursday

to enrich your life: April

to improve your life: Blue Moon

to preserve life: first hour after sunrise on Sunday/first hour after sunset on Wednesday

Longevity

Monday/Saturday/first hour after sunrise on Saturday/first hour after sunset on Tuesday/April/Libra/Capricorn

Love

Dawn/Monday/Thursday/Friday/first hour after sunrise on Monday, Wednesday, or Friday/first hour after sunset on Monday, Thursday, or Saturday/Waxing Year/New Moon/Waxing Moon/Full Moon (especially in March, May, October, and November)/Blue Moon/Summer/April/May/June/October/Taurus/Libra/Capricorn

earthy love: Taurus

idealistic love: Libra

initiation into the mysteries of love: first hour after sunrise on Friday/first hour after sunset on Monday *lovers:* (see People)

married love: first hour after sunrise on Friday/first hour after sunset on Monday

maternal love: first hour after sunrise on Monday/first hour after sunset on Thursday/Cancer

passionate love: Taurus

paternal love: Cancer

physical love: first hour after sunrise on Friday/first hour after sunset on Monday

platonic love: Virgo

the power of love: first hour after sunrise on Friday/first hour after sunset on Monday

profane love: first hour after sunrise on Friday/first hour after sunset on Monday

romantic love: Friday/Libra

sensual love: Taurus

sexual love: Tuesday/first hour after sunrise on Friday/first hour after sunset on Monday/Scorpio

to attract love: Waxing Year/first hour after sunrise on Friday/first hour after sunset on Monday/New Moon

to attract love from women: Thursday

to encourage males to love females: Friday

to invite love: Waxing Moon

Magick (see also Spells)

Midnight/Wednesday/Saturday/first hour after sunrise on Monday or Wednesday/first hour after sunset on Thursday or Saturday/Full Moon (especially in March)/Cancer

aggressive magick: first hour after sunrise on Tuesday/first hour after sunset on Friday

Air magick: Dawn/first hour after sunrise on Wednesday or Thursday/first hour after sunset on Saturday or Sunday/Spring/Full Moon in February/Gemini/Libra/Aquarius

animal magick: Waxing Crescent Moon/Full Moon in June, July, or August

battlefield magick: first hour after sunrise on Tuesday/first hour after sunset on Friday

calendar magick: first hour after sunrise on Monday/first hour after sunset on Thursday

candle magick: Midnight

cat magick: Leo

Crone magick: Waning Moon/Dark Moon/Autumn/Winter/Full Moon in September

deosil magick: Dawn/Waxing Year/Waxing Moon

dragon magick: first hour after sunrise on Tuesday/first hour after sunset on Friday/Spring/Full Moon in May

dream magick: Friday/Winter/Full Moon in May

Earth magick: Midnight/Waxing Moon/Full Moon in May or September/Winter/Taurus/Virgo/Capricorn *elemental magick:* Waxing Moon

fairy magick: May/June/Full Moon in May/Sidhe Moon

female magick: first hour after sunrise on Monday/first hour after sunset on Thursday/Full Moon in May

female sex magick: first hour after sunrise on Friday/first hour after sunset on Monday

Fire magick: Noon/first hour after sunrise on Sunday, Tuesday, or Thursday/first hour after sunset on Wednesday, Friday, or Sunday/Summer/ Aries/Leo/Sagittarius

flower magick: Friday/Spring/May/Full Moon in April, May, or June

garden magick: first hour after sunrise on Friday/first hour after sunset on Monday/Spring/May

hearth magick: Full Moon in October or November

herbal magick: Friday/August/Full Moon in August

horse magick: Sagittarius

ice magick (depends on where you live; use personal judgment): Winter/Full Moon in January or February

incense magick: Friday/first hour after sunrise on Friday/first hour after sunset on Monday

lunar magick: Monday/Thursday/first hour after sunrise on Monday/ first hour after sunset on Thursday/Full Moon/July/Cancer

magickal energy: Dawn/Sunset/Sunday/first hour after sunrise on Sunday/first hour after sunset on Wednesday/Full Moon/Summer

magickal knowledge: first hour after sunrise on Saturday/first hour after sunset on Tuesday *magickal power(s):* first hour after sunrise on Monday or Wednesday/first hour after sunset on Thursday or Saturday/Full Moon/Scorpio

male magick: first hour after sunrise on Sunday/first hour after sunset on Wednesday/Full Moon in June or December

male sex magick: first hour after sunrise on Tuesday/first hour after sunset on Friday

maximum magickal power: Full Moon

mirror magick: Sunset/first hour after sunrise on Friday/first hour after sunset on Monday

night magick: Night/first hour after sunrise on Monday/first hour after sunset on Thursday/Scorpio

positive attitude: Cancer

positive change(s): Waxing Moon/Sagittarius

positive energy: first hour after sunrise on Sunday or Tuesday/first hour after sunset on Wednesday or Friday

positive magick: Dawn/Waxing Moon/Waxing Year/Full Moon in May, June, July, or December

positiveness: first hour after sunrise on Sunday/first hour after sunset on Wednesday

power of positive energy to overcome negative energy: Februrary

seasonal magick: first hour after sunrise on Sunday/first hour after sunset on Wednesday

seed magick: Full Moon in March, April, or May

sex magick: Midnight/Scorpio

snow magick (depends on where you live; use personal judgment): Winter/ Full Moon in January or February

solar magick: Noon/Sunday/first hour after sunrise on Sunday/first hour after sunset on Wednesday

trance magick: Autumn

tree magick: Full Moon in May

triple magick: first hour after sunrise on Monday/first hour after sunset on Thursday

voice magick: first hour after sunrise on Wednesday/first hour after sunset on Saturday/Taurus

Water magick: Sunset/Monday/first hour after sunrise on Monday, Friday, or Saturday/first hour after sunset on Monday, Tuesday, or Thursday/Autumn/Cancer/Scorpio/Aquarius/Pisces

weather magick (depends on where you live; use personal judgment): Thursday/Full Moon in February, March, April, July, or November

widdershins magick: Sunset/Waning Year/Waning Moon

wish magick: Sunday/January/Blue Moon

to balance positive and negative forces: Libra

to begin any magickal operation: Sunday

to charge magickal tools: Waxing Year

to gather/harvest magickal plants: Dawn/Waxing Moon

to open to lunar magick: first hour after sunrise on Monday/first hour after sunset on Thursday

to plan magickal workings: Wednesday

to plant magickal gardens: Spring

to recharge magickal batteries: Void of Course Moon

Marriage

Tuesday/Friday/first hour after sunrise on Tuesday, Thursday, or Friday/first hour after sunset on Sunday, Monday, or Friday/Summer/June/Libra

marriage counselors: Libra

married love: first hour after sunrise on Friday/first hour after sunset on Monday

to encourage marriage: Friday

to work on marriages: Cancer

Meditation

Dawn/Sunset/Monday/Saturday/first hour after sunrise on Monday, Thursday or Friday/first hour after sunset on Monday, Thursday, or Sunday/New Moon/Disseminating Moon/Waning Crescent Moon/Void of Course Moon/Full Moon in July or August/Winter/July/August

deep meditation: Dark Moon

to meditate on the lessons of the previous calendar year: January

to meditate on the power of goodness to overcome evil: February

to meditate on the power of light to overcome darkness: February *to meditate on the power of positive energy to overcome negative energy:* February

to meditate on your accomplishments: Disseminating Moon

to meditate on your motives: Full Moon

Money (see also Financial Matters)

Noon/Sunday/Wednesday/Thursday/Friday/Saturday/first hour after sunrise on Wednesday, Thursday or Friday/first hour after sunset on Saturday, Sunday, or Monday/Waxing Moon/ Full Moon/Autumn/Taurus/Gemini

debt(s): Saturday/first hour after sunrise on Wednesday or Saturday/first hour after sunset on Tuesday or Saturday

income: Friday

personal income: first hour after sunrise on Friday/first hour after sunset on Monday

to attract money: Sunday/Friday/first hour after sunrise on Sunday/first hour after sunset on Wednesday/Full Moon

to borrow money: Leo/Aquarius/Pisces

to hold on to money: Dry Moon

to increase money: Waxing Moon

to increase personal income: Waxing Year

to save money: Taurus/Scorpio/Capricorn

Negativity

Capricorn

negative emotions: first hour after sunrise on Monday/first hour after sunset on Thursday

negative thoughts: Saturday

the power of positive energy to overcome negative energy: February

to avert negative energy: June

to avert negativity: Saturday

to banish negative/bad habits: Waning Year

to banish negative forces: Saturday

to balance negative forces with positive forces: Libra

to banish negative influences: Saturday/Waning Moon

to banish negativity: Tuesday/Thursday/first hour after sunrise on Sunday/first hour after sunset on Wednesday

to banish negativity of the previous calendar year: January

to banish negative thoughts: Full Moon in November

to bind negative forces: Saturday/first hour after sunrise on Saturday/first hour after sunset on Tuesday

to bind negative influences: Saturday

to break negative/bad habits: first hour after sunrise on Wednesday/first hour after sunset on Saturday

to clear negative vibrations: Full Moon in November

to clear negativity: July

to end negative/bad habits: first hour after sunrise on Saturday/first hour after sunset on Tuesday/Waning Moon/Aquarius

to neutralize negativity: Saturday

to protect against negativity: first hour after sunrise on Saturday/first hour after sunset on Tuesday

to reject negativity: Dark Moon

to release negative attachments: Waning Moon

to release negative situations: Waning Moon

to transform negative emotions into compassion: Virgo

to weaken negative influences: Waning Year

to winnow negative people: Waning Moon

Opening (s)

Dawn/first hour after sunrise on Sunday/first hour after sunset on Wednesday/Waxing Crescent Moon

to look for openings: April

to open doors: Thursday

to open locks or bolts: Wednesday

to open minds: Aquarius

to open to lunar magick: first hour after sunrise on Monday/first hour after sunset on Thursday

to open your mind: Gemini

to open your third eye: July

Opportunity

Thursday

opportunism/opportunists: Capricorn

to take advantage of opportunities: April

Organization

January/Waxing Crescent Moon/Full Moon in September/ September/January/Taurus/Virgo/Capricorn

organizational ability: Capricorn

reorganization: Pisces

to get organized: Capricorn

Overcoming

Dawn/Waxing Year/Waxing Moon

to meditate on the power of light to overcome darkness, the power of positive energy to overcome negative energy, and the power of goodness to overcome evil: February

to overcome addictions: first hour after sunrise on Wednesday/first hour after sunset on Saturday

to overcome barriers: March

to overcome blockages: Saturday

to overcome creative blocks: first hour after sunrise on Monday/first hour after sunset on Thursday *to overcome darkness:* Dawn/first hour after sunrise on Sunday/first hour after sunset on Wednesday/Waxing Year

to overcome death: first hour after sunrise on Sunday/first hour after sunset on Wednesday

to overcome disabilities: Sunday

to overcome diseases: Saturday/Waning Moon

to overcome enemies: Tuesday

to overcome limitations: Saturday

to overcome mental blocks: Gemini

to overcome obstacles: Saturday/Waxing Moon/Aries/Capricorn

to overcome personal pride: first hour after sunrise on Sunday/first hour after sunset on Wednesday

to overcome psychic attack: first hour after sunrise on Tuesday/first hour after sunset on Friday

to overcome those who restrict you: Saturday

Passion

Tuesday/Friday/first hour after sunrise on Tuesday or Friday/ first hour after sunset on Monday or Friday/Summer/May/ Aries/Taurus/Leo/Scorpio/Sagittarius

angry passion: first hour after sunrise on Tuesday/first hour after sunset on Friday

emotional passion: first hour after sunrise on Tuesday/first hour after sunset on Friday/Aries *passionate creativity:* Waxing Moon

passionate love: Taurus

physical passion: first hour after sunrise on Friday/first hour after sunset on Monday/Taurus

sensual passion: first hour after sunrise on Friday/first hour after sunset on Monday

sexual passion: first hour after sunrise on Friday/first hour after sunset on Monday

Past-life Work (see also Reincarnation)

Monday/Saturday/Winter/Pisces

Peace

Monday/Wednesday/Friday/Saturday/first hour after sunrise on Monday, Friday, or Saturday/first hour after sunset on Monday, Tuesday, or Thursday/Full Moon in April or May/February/August/Taurus/Libra

inner peace: Taurus

peace activists: Cancer

peace and quiet: Libra

People

Friday

power over other people: Leo

to free yourself from the control of other people: Full Moon in December

to inspire other people: Leo

to limit the actions of other people: Saturday/first hour after sunrise on Saturday/first hour after sunset on Tuesday

to limit the freedom of other people: Saturday

to meet new people: April

to visit people: Wednesday

to work with other people: Leo

ACTIVISTS
Aquarius

peace activists: Cancer

AUTHORITY FIGURES
Sunday/Thursday/first hour after sunrise on Sunday or Thursday/first hour after sunset on Sunday or Wednesday

commanders: Leo

high-ranking military officers: first hour after sunrise on Tuesday/first hour after sunset on Friday *rulers:* first hour after sunrise on Sunday or Thursday/first hour after sunset on Wednesday or Sunday

❧

BABIES
first hour after sunrise on Monday/first hour after sunset on Thursday/Cancer

to protect babies: Waxing Crescent Moon

❧

BUSINESS PEOPLE
Sunday/Tuesday/first hour after sunrise on Wednesday/first hour after sunset on Saturday

entrepreneurs: Aries

industrialists: first hour after sunrise on Wednesday/first hour after sunset on Saturday/Taurus

merchants: Wednesday/Thursday

realtors: Saturday/Taurus

traders: Thursday

❧

CHILDREN
Sunday/Monday/first hour after sunrise on Sunday, Monday, Wednesday, or Friday/first hour after sunset on Monday, Wednesday, Thursday, or Saturday/Full Moon/Cancer/Leo

adolescents: first hour after sunrise on Friday/first hour after sunset on Monday

to protect children: first hour after sunrise on Monday/first hour after sunset on Thursday/Full Moon in November

❧

COMMUNICATORS
Gemini

broadcasters: Thursday

critics: Wednesday

interpreters: first hour after sunrise on Wednesday/first hour after sunset on Saturday

media personalities: Gemini

PR specialists: Gemini

publicists: Thursday

public speakers: Wednesday

publishers: Thursday

❧

COMPETITORS
Tuesday/first hour after sunrise on Tuesday/first hour after sunset on Friday

athletes (including fighters): Tuesday/first hour after sunrise on Tuesday/first hour after sunset on Friday

archers: Sagittarius

gymnasts: first hour after sunrise on Wednesday/first hour after sunset on Saturday *wrestlers:* first hour after sunrise on Wednesday/first hour after sunset on Saturday

❧

CONTESTANTS
Tuesday

debaters: Tuesday

warriors: Tuesday/first hour after sunrise on Tuesday/first hour after sunset on Friday/Aries

❧

CREATIVE PEOPLE

architects: Friday/first hour after sunrise on Saturday/first hour after sunset on Tuesday/Taurus/Capricorn

artists: Wednesday/Friday/Taurus/Libra/Pisces

composers: first hour after sunrise on Friday/first hour after sunset on Monday

designers: Friday/Libra

editors: Wednesday

hairstylists: Friday

journalists: Wednesday/Gemini

makeup artists: Friday/Libra

painters: Friday

poets: Wednesday/Friday/Pisces

sculptors: Friday/Taurus

writers: Wednesday/first hour after sunrise on Wednesday/first hour after sunset on Saturday/Gemini/Sagittarius

visual artists: Wednesday/first hour after sunrise on Friday/first hour after sunset on Monday

CRIMINALS
Saturday

con artists: first hour after sunrise on Wednesday/first hour after sunset on Saturday

murderers: Saturday

stalkers: Saturday

thieves: Monday/Thursday/first hour after sunrise on Wednesday/first hour after sunset on Saturday

to protect against thieves: first hour after sunrise on Wednesday/first hour after sunset on Saturday

DEPRESSED PEOPLE
First hour after sunrise on Saturday/first hour after sunset on Tuesday

DIVORCED PEOPLE
Waning Moon

EDUCATORS
Wednesday/Sagittarius

professors: Sagittarius

teachers: Wednesday/first hour after sunrise on Wednesday/first hour after sunset on Saturday

❧

EMPLOYERS
Sunday/Thursday

❧

ENTHUSIASTS
Tuesday

❧

ENEMIES
first hour after sunrise on Tuesday/first hour after sunset on Friday/Waning Moon/Dark Moon

power over enemies: Tuesday

to appease enemies: Thursday

to defeat enemiese: Tuesday

to move openly against enemies: Tuesday

to move secretly against enemies: Saturday

to overcome enemies: Tuesday

to repel enemies: Waning Year

❧

EXPLORERS
Aries/Sagittarius

❧

FAMILY MEMBERS
Monday/Wednesday/Full Moon/Cancer

brothers: Sunday

fathers: Sunday/first hour after sunrise on Saturday or Sunday/first hour after sunset on Tuesday or Wednesday/Capricorn

grandparents: first hour after sunrise on Saturday/first hour after sunset on Tuesday

husbands: Sunday/first hour after sunrise on Sunday/first hour after sunset on Wednesday

mothers: Monday/first hour after sunrise on Monday/first hour after sunset on Thursday/Full Moon/Cancer

siblings: Wednesday

sisters: Monday

spouses: first hour after sunrise on Friday/first hour after sunset on Monday

to protect nursing mothers: Waxing Crescent Moon

wives: Monday

FAMOUS PEOPLE
Sunday/first hour after sunrise on Thursday/first hour after sunset on Sunday

prominent persons: Capricorn

❧

FINANCIAL PEOPLE

accountants: Wednesday/Virgo

bankers: Sunday/first hour after sunrise on Saturday/first hour after sunset on Tuesday

financial planners: Virgo

treasurers: first hour after sunrise on Saturday/first hour after sunset on Tuesday

❧

FRIENDS

Monday/Friday/first hour after sunrise on Friday/first hour after sunset on Monday/Leo

❧

HEALERS

chiropractors: Friday

dentists: Saturday/first hour after sunrise on Tuesday/first hour after sunset on Friday/Scorpio

doctors: Monday/first hour after sunrise on Tuesday/first hour after sunset on Friday/Thursday

midwives: first hour after sunrise on Monday/first hour after sunset on Thursday

nurses: Monday/first hour after sunrise on Monday/first hour after sunset on Thursday/Virgo

psychiatrists: Scorpio

psychologists: Monday/Thursday

surgeons: Tuesday/first hour after sunrise on Tuesday/first hour after sunset on Friday

❧

INFLUENTIAL PEOPLE
First hour after sunrise on Thursday/first hour after sunset on Sunday

chiefs of staff: first hour after sunrise on Monday/first hour after sunset on Thursday

politicians: Tuesday/Thursday/first hour after sunrise on Thursday/first hour after sunset on Sunday/Capricorn

power brokers: first hour after sunrise on Thursday/first hour after sunset on Sunday

statesmen: Libra

to influence people in high places: Thursday

❧

INTELLECTUALS
Wednesday/first hour after sunrise on Thursday/first hour after sunset on Sunday/Aquarius

historians: first hour after sunrise on Saturday/first hour after sunset on Tuesday

philosophers: Thursday/first hour after sunrise on Thursday/first hour after sunset on Sunday/Sagittarius

❧

INVESTIGATORS
Scorpio

detectives: Scorpio

researchers: Thursday/Scorpio/Aquarius

❧

LAW ENFORCERS:
First hour after sunrise on Tuesday/first hour after sunset on Friday

corrections officers: Saturday/first hour after sunrise on Tuesday or Saturday/first hour after sunset on Tuesday or Friday

judges: Sunday/first hour after sunrise on Thursday/first hour after sunset on Sunday/Libra

lawyers: Tuesday/Libra

police officers: Tuesday/first hour after sunrise on Tuesday/first hour after sunset on Friday

prosecutors: Saturday

❧

LEADERS
Sunday/first hour after sunrise on Sunday or Thursday/first hour after sunset on Sunday or Wednesday/Leo

corporate leaders: Capricorn

religious leaders: first hour after sunrise on Thursday/first hour after sunset on Sunday

world leaders: Sunday

༄

LOVERS
Friday/first hour after sunrise on Friday/first hour after sunset on Monday/Full Moon (especially in June)

༄

MANAGERS
administrators: Sagittarius

CEOs: first hour after sunrise on Sunday/first hour after sunset on Wednesday

executive assistants: first hour after sunrise on Monday/first hour after sunset on Thursday

executives: first hour after sunrise on Thursday/first hour after sunset on Sunday

༄

MARINERS/SAILORS/FISHERFOLK
First hour after sunrise on Monday/first hour after sunset on Thursday

༄

MEN
Sunday/first hour after sunrise on Sunday or Tuesday/first hour after sunset on Wednesday or Friday

old men: first hour after sunrise on Saturday/first hour after sunset on Tuesday

❧

MESSENGERS
First hour after sunrise on Monday/first hour after sunset on Thursday

❧

MISSING PERSONS
Saturday

❧

NEIGHBORS
Wednesday

❧

OLD PEOPLE
Saturday/Waning Moon/first hour after sunrise on Saturday/first hour after sunset on Tuesday

❧

PARTNERS
Tuesday/Friday/first hour after sunrise on Friday/first hour after sunset on Monday/Libra

couples: Libra

female partners: Monday

male partners: Sunday

soul mates: Friday

❦

PERFORMERS
Sunday/first hour after sunrise on Sunday/first hour after sunset on Wednesday/Leo

actors: Sunday/Leo

comedians: first hour after sunrise on Wednesday/first hour after sunset on Saturday

dancers: Friday

entertainers: Friday

musicians: Wednesday/Friday/first hour after sunrise on Friday/first hour after sunset on Monday/Pisces

singers: Taurus

❦

PSYCHICS
Monday/Full Moon/Pisces

❦

SCIENTISTS
Wednesday/first hour after sunrise on Wednesday/first hour after sunset on Saturday/Capricorn/Aquarius

❦

SPORTS FANS
Thursday

❧

STRANGERS

First hour after sunrise on Friday/first hour after sunset on Monday

❧

STUDENTS

Wednesday

❧

TRAVELERS

Monday/Wednesday/first hour after sunrise on Monday/first hour after sunset on Thursday/Sagittarius

to protect travelers: first hour after sunrise on Monday or Thursday/first hour after sunset on Thursday or Sunday

❧

WOMEN

Monday/first hour after sunrise on Monday or Friday/first hour after sunset on Monday or Thursday

Crones: Waning Moon

post-menopausal women: Waning Moon

pregnant women: Full Moon

❧

YOUNG PEOPLE

Tuesday/Wednesday/first hour after sunrise on Friday/first hour after sunset on Monday

Problems

female problems: Friday

legal problems: first hour after sunrise on Thursday/first hour after sunset on Sunday

to cause problems: Saturday

to end problems: Waning Moon

to get a new angle on a problem: Dawn/New Moon

to settle personal problems: Full Moon in January

to settle problems: first hour after sunrise on Thursday/first hour after sunset on Sunday

to settle serious problems: Wednesday

to solve problems: first hour after sunrise on Monday/first hour after sunset on Thursday/Full Moon/Aquarius

Projects

Dawn

artistic projects: Full Moon

new financial projects: Aries

new projects: New Moon

to begin projects: March

to conclude/finish projects: Full Moon/February/September

to tend projects: July

Prosperity

Sunday/Thursday/Friday/first hour after sunrise on Sunday or Thursday/first hour after sunset on Sunday or Wednesday/Waxing Moon/Full Moon (especially in March, April, May, June, August, October, or December)/March/Taurus/Leo/Capricorn

to attract prosperity: first hour after sunrise on Thursday or Friday/first hour after sunset on Sunday or Monday

to create prosperity: first hour after sunrise on Thursday/first hour after sunset on Sunday

Protection

Noon/Sunday/Monday/Tuesday/Thursday/Saturday/first hour after sunrise on Sunday, Tuesday, or Saturday/first hour after sunset on Tuesday, Wednesday, or Friday/Waxing Moon/Waning Moon/Disseminating Moon/Full Moon (especially in January, March, May, June, July, August, September, October, or November)/Blue Moon/Summer/January/February/May/June/August

protectiveness: Cancer

to create a shield of protection: New Moon

to protect against conspiracy: first hour after sunrise on Saturday/first hour after sunset on Tuesday

to protect against diseases and disorders: first hour after sunrise on Sunday/first hour after sunset on Wednesday

to protect against negativity: first hour after sunrise on Saturday/first hour after sunset on Tuesday *to protect against poisoning:* first hour after sunrise on Saturday/first hour after sunset on Tuesday

to protect against poverty: Full Moon in January

to protect against theft/thieves: first hour after sunrise on Wednesday/first hour after sunset on Saturday

to protect babies: Waxing Crescent Moon

to protect children: (see People)

to protect cows: Waxing Crescent Moon

to protect the home: Full Moon in October/Blue Moon

to protect nursing mothers: Waxing Crescent Moon

to protect travelers: (see People)

Psychic Work

Sunday/Monday/first hour after sunrise on Monday or Thursday/first hour after sunset on Sunday or Thursday/Full Moon (especially in June or July)/July/October/Cancer/Pisces

clairvoyance: Monday/first hour after sunrise on Monday/first hour after sunset on Thursday/Full Moon in February/Scorpio/Sagittarius/Pisces

ESP: Aquarius/Pisces

psychic ability: Monday/Full Moon/Saturday/Aquarius

psychic awareness: Monday/first hour after sunrise on Monday/first hour after sunset on Thursday/Waxing Moon/Spring/Scorpio/Pisces *psychic connections:* Pisces

psychic defense: first hour after sunrise on Saturday/first hour after sunset on Tuesday

psychic development: first hour after sunrise on Monday/first hour after sunset on Thursay/Full Moon in September

psychic dreams: first hour after sunrise on Monday/first hour after sunset on Thursday/Pisces

psychic energy: Full Moon/Cancer/Scorpio/Pisces

psychic growth: Scorpio

psychic increase: first hour after sunrise on Monday/first hour after sunset on Thursday/Waxing Moon

psychic messages: Capricorn

psychic power(s): first hour after sunrise on Monday/first hour after sunset on Thursday/Scorpio

psychic self-defense: Saturday

psychic sensitivity: first hour after sunrise on Monday/first hour after sunset on Thursday/Cancer/Aquarius

psychics: Monday/Full Moon/Pisces

telepathy: Capricorn/Pisces

to increase psychic ability: Full Moon

to increase psychic awareness: first hour after sunrise on Saturday/first hour after sunset on Tuesday

to overcome psychic attack: first hour after sunrise on Tuesday/first hour after sunset on Friday

Purification

Dawn/Sunday/Tuesday/first hour after sunrise on Saturday/ first hour after sunset on Tuesday/Full Moon (especially in January, February, or November)/Spring/February/Virgo/Scorpio

spiritual purification: February

to purify an athame: Waning Moon

to purify crystals, objects, or stones: first hour after sunrise on Sunday or Monday/first hour after sunset on Wednesday or Thursday

Reincarnation (see also Past-life Work)

Monday/Saturday/first hour after sunrise on Monday/first hour after sunset on Thursday/October/Full Moon in October

Relationships

Friday/first hour after sunrise on Friday/first hour after sunset on Monday/Full Moon/Gemini

new relationships: Dawn/New Moon

to hold on to relationships: Dry Moon

to strengthen relationships: Waxing Year/Waxing Moon

Releasing

Dawn/New Moon/Full Moon in October/Waning Moon/ Wet Moon/October/November/Pisces *emotional release:* February

to release the dead: Saturday

to release negative attachments: Waning Moon

to release negative situations: Waning Moon

to release the past: January

to release spirits: Wednesday

to release things that no longer serve you well: Full Moon in October

Reversal

Sunset/Wednesday/Saturday/Waning Moon/January/Full Moon in January

Ritual(s)

Air rituals: Dawn/first hour after sunrise on Wednesday or Thursday/ first hour after sunset on Saturday or Sunday/Spring/Full Moon in February/Gemini/Libra/Aquarius

Earth rituals: Midnight/Waxing Moon/Full Moon in May or September/Winter/Taurus/Virgo/Capricorn

female rituals: Friday/first hour after sunrise on Friday/first hour after sunset on Monday

Fire rituals: Noon/first hour after sunrise on Sunday, Tuesday, or Thursday/first hour after sunset on Wednesday, Friday, or Sunday/Summer/Aries/Leo/Sagittarius *male rituals:* Tuesday/first hour after sunrise on Tuesday/first hour after sunset on Friday

sea rituals: Monday/first hour after sunrise on Monday/first hour after sunset on Thursday

to boost ritual energy: Sunday/first hour after sunrise on Sunday/first hour after sunset on Wednesday

to increase the effectiveness of rituals: Full Moon

Water rituals: Sunset/Monday/first hour after sunrise on Monday, Friday, or Saturday/first hour after sunset on Monday, Tuesday, or Thursday/Autumn/Cancer/Scorpio/Aquarius/Pisces

Sex

Tuesday/Friday/first hour after sunrise on Tuesday or Friday/first hour after sunset on Friday or Monday/Full Moon (especially in May, June, July, and September)/May/Aries/Taurus/Leo/Scorpio

sex drive/libido: first hour after sunrise on Tuesday/first hour after sunset on Friday/Aries/Leo

sex glands: Scorpio

sex magick: (see Magick)

sexual advances: first hour after sunrise on Tuesday or Friday/first hour after sunset on Monday or Friday

sexual energy: first hour after sunrise on Sunday, Tuesday, or Friday/first hour after sunset on Monday, Wednesday, or Friday/Scorpio

sexual freedom: May

sexual healing: first hour after sunrise on Friday/first hour after sunset on Monday

sexual love: Tuesday/first hour after sunrise on Friday/first hour after sunset on Monday/Scorpio

sexual matters: Scorpio

sexual need: first hour after sunrise on Friday/first hour after sunset on Monday

sexual passion: first hour after sunrise on Friday/first hour after sunset on Monday

sexual power: first hour after sunrise on Friday/first hour after sunset on Monday/Scorpio

sexual union: first hour after sunrise on Friday/first hour after sunset on Monday

sexually transmitted diseases: first hour after sunrise on Friday/first hour after sunset on Monday

Sexuality

Friday/first hour after sunrise on Friday/first hour after sunset on Monday/Full Moon/Scorpio/Sagittarius

female sexuality: first hour after sunrise on Friday/first hour after sunset on Monday

male sexuality: first hour after sunrise on Tuesday/first hour after sunset on Friday

to control sexuality: Virgo

Spells (see also Magick)

First hour after sunrise on Monday/first hour after sunset on Thursday

Air spells: Dawn/first hour after sunrise on Wednesday or Thursday/first hour after sunset on Saturday or Sunday/Spring/Full Moon in February/Gemini/Libra/Aquarius

cauldron spells: first hour after sunrise on Monday/first hour after sunset on Thursday/Full Moon

Earth spells: Midnight/Waxing Moon/Full Moon in May or September/Winter/Taurus/Virgo/Capricorn

Fire spells: Noon/first hour after sunrise on Sunday, Tuesday, or Thursday/first hour after sunset on Wednesday, Friday, or Sunday/Summer/Aries/Leo/Sagittarius

sea rituals/spells: first hour after sunrise on Monday/first hour after sunset on Thursday/Monday

to begin spells: Waxing Moon

to empower spells: Sunrise/Full Moon

to energize spells: first hour after sunrise on Friday/first hour after sunset on Monday

to strengthen the effectiveness of spells: Full Moon

Water spells: Sunset/Monday/first hour after sunrise on Monday, Friday, or Saturday/first hour after sunset on Monday, Tuesday, or Thursday/Autumn/Cancer/Scorpio/Aquarius/Pisces

wind spells: Full Moon in March, April, or June/whenever it is windiest where you live

Stability

Saturday/first hour after sunrise on Saturday or Sunday/first hour after sunset on Tuesday or Wednesday/New Moon/Taurus/Leo/Virgo/Scorpio/Capricorn/Aquarius

instability: Gemini

Strength

Sunday/Tuesday/first hour after sunrise on Sunday or Tuesday/first hour after sunset on Wednesday or Friday/Summer/June/Aries/Taurus/Leo

matriarchal strength: Waxing Crescent Moon

physical strength: Sunday/Tuesday/first hour after sunrise on Tuesday/first hour after sunset on Friday/Sagittarius

strength in conflict: Tuesday

strength through persistence and endurance: first hour after sunrise on Saturday/first hour after sunset on Tuesday

strong emotions: Leo

to grow strong: June

to strengthen: Waxing Year

to strengthen purpose: Taurus

to strengthen relationships: Waxing Year

Study

Dawn/Wednesday/Thursday/first hour after sunrise on Wednesday/first hour after sunset on Saturday/Sagittarius/Capricorn

students: Wednesday

Success

Sunday/Thursday/Friday/first hour after sunrise on Sunday or Thursday/first hour after sunset on Sunday or Wednesday/Waxing Moon/Full Moon in July/March/July/Scorpio/Capricorn

business success: Dawn/Virgo

material success: Thursday

professional success: Sunday

to invite success: Waxing Year

total success: first hour after sunrise on Sunday/first hour after sunset on Wednesday

Transformation

Sunset/Saturday/first hour after sunrise on Monday/first hour after sunset on Thursday/New Moon/Full Moon (especially in November and December)/Waning Moon/Autumn/October/November/Scorpio

to transform negative emotions into compassion: Virgo

Travel

Monday/Wednesday/first hour after sunrise on Sunday, Monday or Wednesday/first hour after sunset on Wednesday, Thursday or Saturday/Full Moon/Gemini/Sagittarius

travelers: (see People)

business travel: Sagittarius

long-distance travel: Thursday

night travel: first hour after sunrise on Sunday or Monday/first hour after sunset on Wednesday or Thursday

pleasure trips: Waxing Moon/Gemini/Leo/Aquarius

travel by water: first hour after sunrise on Monday/first hour after sunset on Thursday

Unbinding

Waxing Moon/Full Moon

Uncrossing

Wednesday/first hour after sunrise on Saturday/first hour after sunset on Tuesday/Gemini

Understanding

Wednesday/Friday/Saturday/Full Moon/Waning Crescent Moon/November/Virgo *group understanding:* Aquarius

spiritual understanding: Dark Moon

to awaken understanding: first hour after sunrise on Sunday/first hour after sunset on Wednesday

to understand your dark side: Dark Moon

to understand yourself: October

Vision Quests

Summer/Dark Moon/March/Full Moon in February or December

Visualization

Dawn/Sunset/Spring

Weather

Depends on where you live; use personal judgment.

nourishing rain: Spring

rain: first hour after sunrise on Monday/first hour after sunset on Thursday/Wet Moon

storms: February/Full Moon in February, March, or November

to call storms: March

weather divination: January

weather magick: (see Magick)

wind: Full Moon in March, April, or June/whenever it is windiest where you live

Will

Sunday/Saturday/first hour after sunrise on Sunday or Tuesday/first hour after sunset on Wednesday or Friday/Summer/Leo

good will: Virgo

to surrender to divine will: Wednesday

to use will properly: Full Moon

Willpower

Sunday/first hour after sunrise on Sunday/first hour after sunset on Wednesday/Aries/Leo/Scorpio

Wisdom

Sunday/Wednesday/Saturday/first hour after sunrise on Saturday, Sunday, Wednesday, or Thursday/first hour after sunset on Tuesday, Wednesday, Saturday, or Sunday/Full Moon (especially in July, September, or December)/Waning Moon/Dark Moon/September/Scorpio/Sagittarius/Capricorn

clarity leading to wisdom: New Moon

inner eye of wisdom: first hour after sunrise on Monday/first hour after sunset on Thursday *inner wisdom:* first hour after sunrise on Monday/first hour after sunset on Thursday/Full Moon

lunar wisdom: first hour after sunrise on Monday/first hour after sunset on Thursday

sacred wisdom: first hour after sunrise on Saturday/first hour after sunset on Tuesday

wisdom leading to illumination: Waxing Crescent Moon

wisdom of rebirth: first hour after sunrise on Wednesday/first hour after sunset on Saturday

Glossary

❧ Glossary of Terms and Mythological Figures

Achilles: (Greek) A hero who fought in the Trojan War.

Aegipan: (Greek) A god who took the form of a goat with the tail of a fish. Some call him Goat-Pan and consider him an aspect of the god Pan. Aegipan became the constellation Capricorn.

Aerope: (Greek) The mother of Agamemnon.

Agamemnon: (Greek) The king who led Greek forces during the Trojan War.

Agathos Daimon: (Greek) An androgynous spirit that is benevolent and protective.

Agrat Bat Mahalat: (Hebrew) Female spirit of uncleanness (sexuality).

Ahriman: (Persian) The prince of demons. He is also called Angra Mainyu.

Amalthea: (Greek) A goat that suckled the infant Zeus in a cave.

Amazon: (Greek) A legendary female warrior. Amazons are said to have lived in all-female societies, gone into battle on horses, and removed their right breasts to facilitate their skills as archers.

Angel: I. (Judeo-Christian) A winged celestial being. Specific angels include Adabiel, Adnachiel, Agiel, Amabael, Amabiel, Amatiel, Ambriel, Anael, Araziel, Asasiel, Attarib, Azazel, Barbiel, Barchiel, Cael, Cambiel,

Caracasa, Cassiel, Cetarari, Commissoros, Core, Dardiel, Elimiel, Gabriel, Gargatel, Gaviel, Gazardiel, Guabarel, Hadakiel, Hagiel, Hamaliel, Hanael, Haniel, Hasdiel, Hurtapel, Hyniel, Iaqwiel, Ichadriel, Iophiel, Machatan, Machidiel, Madimiel, Maion, Michael, Miel, Milkiel, Muriel, Orifiel, Raphael, Rashiel, Richol, Sachiel, Samael, Satael, Semeliel, Seraphiel, Seratiel, Tariel, Tarquam, Tiriel, Tsaphiel, Tubiel, Uriel, Verchiel, Voel, Yahriel, Zachariel, Zadkiel, Zaphkiel, Zerachiel, and Zuriel. 2. (Zoroastrian) A winged celestial being. Specific angels include Aban, Azar, Bahman, Chur, Dai, Isfandarmend, Khurdad, Mihr, Shahrivari, and Tir.

Antiope: (Greek) An Amazon; she is the only one known to have been married, to the hero Theseus.

Apis Bull: (Egyptian) A sacred black bull that was housed in a temple in Memphis. He was considered an avatar of the god Ptah until death, when he was assimilated with the god Osiris.

Athame: A ceremonial knife that is used in magick and rituals.

Banshee: (Irish; Bean Sidhe, pronounced "banshee") Female death spirit; ancestral spirit; fairy. The wailing of a banshee means that someone is about to die.

Bean Nighe: (Irish; pronounced "ban-neeyeh") Female water spirit; death spirit; a type of banshee.

Benthesicyme: (Greek) A daughter of the sea deities Poseidon and Amphitrite. Some consider her a sea nymph.

Br'er Rabbit: (African-American) A trickster figure from folktales.

Brownie: (British) A house fairy.

Buddha, the: (Indian) Siddhartha Gautama, a spiritual teacher who achieved enlightenment and founded the Buddhist religion.

Caduceus: (Greek) A wand entwined by two serpents, topped by a winged orb. The caduceus, also called the snake's staff, is the magical staff of the Greek god Hermes. It is also the modern symbol of the medical profession.

Capricornus: (Greek) Aegipan's son, who aided the Olympian gods in their war against the Titans by providing them with great horns with which to make noise.

Cassandra: (Trojan) A daughter of King Priam and Queen Hecuba. She had the gift of prophecy, but was cursed that no one would ever believe her predictions.

Cecrops: (Greek) A king who was the first to offer libations to the gods.

Centaur: (Greek) A mythical being that is human from the waist up and horse from the waist down.

Chakra: An energy node in the human body.

Charon: (Greek) The ferryman who carries the newly dead across the river into Hades.

Chiron: (Greek) A kind, intelligent centaur. He was a skilled healer who healed others, despite suffering great pain from a wound that could not be healed.

Chrysaor: (Greek) A giant; the son of Poseidon and Medusa.

Chrysothemis: (Greek; Cretan) A demigoddess of agriculture.

Corn spirit: A vegetation spirit that has dominion over grain.

Crotus: (Greek) A centaur who invented the hunting bow and the use of rhythmic beats in music.

Daphne: (Greek) A nymph who was transformed into a laurel tree by the goddess Gaia to save her from being raped by the god Apollo.

Delilah: (Hebrew) Samson's wife. She was bribed by the Palestinians to break his strength, and did so by cutting his hair.

Deosil: Clockwise.

Deucalon: (Greek) A man who survived a great flood by building an ark. He and his wife then repopulated the land.

Diarmuid: (Irish; pronounced "der-mot") A warrior who was loved by the goddess Graine. He is also called Diarmuid of the Love Spot because he had a mark on his face that made women fall in love with him.

Dioscuri, the: (Greek) Castor and Polydeuces, twin sons of the god Zeus.

Distaff: A rod attached to a spinning wheel. It is cleft on one end to hold unspun fibers.

Djinn: (Arabian) Nature spirit; spirit of smokeless fire. Djinns (or more properly djinna) are magical beings who are invisible, powerful, may be positive or negative, and can appear to humans in a variety of guises. They are also called genies.

Dryad: (Greek) A wood nymph.

Elektra: (Greek) A daughter of Agamemnon and Clytemnestra. Her name is also spelled Electra.

Endymion: (Greek) A handsome mortal man who was loved by the goddess Selene.

Father Time: (Modern) A personification of time.

Finn Mac Cool: (Irish; Fionn Mac Cumhail, pronounced "fin mak-kool") A legendary hero who was a chieftain, poet, and warrior.

Ganymede: (Greek) A handsome Trojan youth who was loved by the god Zeus. After death, he was granted immortality, made a Cupbearer of the Gods, and placed in the heavens as the constellation Aquarius.

Gawain, Sir: (British) In Arthurian legend, a Knight of the Round Table.

Gilgamesh: (Babylonian) A king of Uruk; the hero of the Epic of Gilgamesh.

Gna: (Norse) An attendant of the goddess Frigg.

Green Knight: (British) A mysterious warrior who challenged Sir Gawain in the Arthurian legends.

Griffin: A mythical creature that has a lion's body and the head and wings of an eagle. Alternate spellings for it include griffon and gryphon.

Guinevere: (British) Arthur's queen, in the Arthurian legends. Arthur held the throne by right of his marriage to her. She took Sir Lancelot as her lover, which was her right as a Celtic queen.

Heliades, the: (Greek) Seven nymphs, daughters of the god Helios.

Herakles Melkarth: (Greco-Roman) The demigod Herakles/Hercules conflated with the Phoenician god Melkarth. Variations of his name include Herakles-Melqart, Hercules Melqart, Hercules Melkarth, Melqart-Hercules, and so on.

Herakles Ogmius: (Romano-Celtic) The demigod Herkales/Hercules conflated with the Celtic god Ogmius. Variations of his name include Heracles Ogmius, Hercules Ogma, and so on.

Hercules: (Roman) Semidivine hero. His Greek name is Herakles.

Hercules Melkarth: (Roman) An aspect of the demigod Hercules.

Hesperides, the: (Greek) Singing sisters who dwell in a beautiful garden, where they guard over the tree that bears the Golden Apples of the gods.

High John the Conqueror: (African-American) Folk hero; a trickster figure who was evoked by slaves to evade their masters. He is also called John the Conqueror.

Holly King: (British) A nature spirit who has dominion over holly plants and the period from Summer Solstice to Winter Solstice; a devolved aspect of the Horned God.

Hyacinthus: (Greek) A flower hero.

Hyades, the: (Greek) A sisterhood of nymphs who bring rain.

Imdugud: (Sumerian) A mythological thunderbird.

Io: (Greek) A priestess of Hera who was seduced by the god Zeus. He then transformed her into a beautiful white cow in an attempt to avoid his wife Hera's jealousy.

Iphigenia: (Greek) A daughter of Agamemnon and Clytemnestra. Her father sacrificed her in order to obtain a favorable wind to launch his fleet for the Trojan War.

Jack Frost: (Modern) Personification of cold winter weather; the elfish Nature spirit who frosts windowpanes.

Jenny Wren: (British) A Nature spirit who has dominion over the period from Summer Solstice to Winter Solstice.

John Barleycorn: (British) A personification of barley crops and the alcoholic beverages distilled from them.

John the Baptist: (Christian) A prophet and cousin of Jesus, who baptized people.

Mab: (British) A night sprite; a fairy queen; a devolved aspect of the Irish goddess Medb.

Maenads, the: (Greek) Female worshipers of the god Dionysus who were known for their violent ecstatic frenzies. They are also called the Raving Ones, and the Wild Women.

Maid Marian: (British) A legendary figure. Originally associated with

Beltane (May Day) celebrations, she later became the companion of Robin Hood.

Manitou: (Algonquin) The spirit of an animal, plant, or thing.

Mary Magdalene: (Christian) A prostitute who became a disciple and possibly the wife and/or priestess of Jesus.

Medusa: (Greek) A once-beautiful woman who was changed into a Gorgon, a winged chthonic being with snakes for hair. Any human who gazed upon her was instantly turned to stone.

Mercury: 1. The planet Mercury. 2. (Roman) God of trade and commerce. 3. A poisonous liquid metal that is also called quicksilver ☠. 4. *Mercurialis perennis*, a rank hairy herb that is also called Dog's Mercury.

Merfolk: Mermaids and mermen; mythical beings that are human from the waist up and fish from the waist down. They are also called merpeople.

Merlin: (British) A great wizard and counselor to King Arthur in the Arthurian legends.

Methuselah: (Hebrew) A patriarch who was noted for his great longevity.

Minotaur: (Greek) A being with the head of a bull and the body of a man.

Mokosha: (Russian) A devolved aspect of the goddess Mokosh that developed after the advent of Christianity. She has a large head, long skinny arms, and comes in darkness to destroy the yarn of spinners who neglect to make the sign of the cross over their work at the end of the day.

Narcissus: (Greek) A flower hero.

Nereid: (Greek) A sea nymph.

Nimuë: (British) A beautiful young woman with whom Merlin became besotted when he was elderly. She learned magic from him, then used it to seal him in an enchanted sleep. Other names for her include Nineve, Niniane, and Vivien. She is also one of the figures who is called the Lady of the Lake.

Nymph: (Greco-Roman) A beautiful female Nature spirit. Nymphs are generally associated with mountains, woods, or bodies of water.

Oak King: (British) A Nature spirit who has dominion over oak trees and the period from Winter Solstice to Summer Solstice; a devolved aspect of the Horned God.

Odysseus: (Greco-Roman) A hero who fought on the Greek side during the Trojan War. He was a trickster figure who created the Trojan Horse. His Roman name is Ulysses.

Okyale: (Greek) An Amazon archer.

Old Man Winter: (Modern) A personification of Winter.

Omphale: (Greek) A Libyan queen to whom Herakles was enslaved for three years.

Palamedes, Sir: (British) A Knight of the Round Table in Arthurian legend.

Pammon: (Trojan) A son of King Priam and Queen Hecuba.

Pandarus: (Greek) A Trojan archer who fought in the Trojan War.

Pasiphaë: (Greek) An Oceanid (sea nymph).

Pegasus: (Greek) A mythical winged horse.

Penelopeia: (Greek) A dryad; mother of the god Pan.

Phaedra: (Greek) Wife of the hero Theseus, who loved his son.

Plant devas: Nature spirits associated with particular flowers, herbs, shrubs, etc.

Pleiades, the: (Greek) A sisterhood of nymphs who are also called the Ladies of Plenty.

Porphyrion: (Greek) A giant.

Praxithea: (Greek) A naiad (freshwater nymph), daughter of the sea deities Oceanus and Tethys.

Reynard the Fox: (European) In folklore, a trickster figure who could always talk his way out of trouble.

Rhode: (Greek) A heliad (sea nymph).

Robin Goodfellow: (British) A mischievous male fairy who is also called Puck; a devolved aspect of the Horned God.

Robin Hood: (British) Legendary outlaw hero of Sherwood Forest, who stole from the rich and gave to the poor.

Robin Redman: (British) Another name for the Oak King.

Romulus and Remus: (Roman) Legendary twin brothers who founded the city of Rome.

Samson: (Hebrew) A fighter whose long hair gave him extraordinary strength. He killed many Palestinians and burned their crops. In return for a bribe from the Palestinians, his wife, Delilah, sapped his strength by cutting his hair. They took Samson prisoner and blinded him. His strength returned when his hair grew back. He then killed himself and many Palestinians by toppling a temple's pillars.

Satan: (Judeo-Christian) A powerfully evil entity; a fallen angel; the chief demon. Other names for him include the Devil, Shaitan, and Prince of Darkness.

Satyr: (Greek) A woodland Nature spirit that has the head and body of a man, with the legs and feet of a goat.

Sea goat: A mythical creature that has the head and forequarters of a goat and the tail of a fish.

Seraph: (Judeo-Christian) Seraphs, or seraphim, are the highest-ranking angels. They are said to have three pairs of wings.

Sidhe: (Irish; pronounced "shee") The fey; the fairy race; fairies.

Sleipnir: (Norse) The magical eight-legged horse of the god Odin.

Snow Queen, the: A fairy-tale character that is based on the Norse goddess Freya.

Suffume: (Archaic) To fumigate from below, especially with aromatic smoke.

Sun Hou-Tzu: (Chinese) A monkey spirit; a trickster figure.

Sylph: (Greek) A nymph of the Air.

Sylvan Spirit: A Nature spirit who dwells in a forest or woodland.

Syn: (Norse) An attendant of the goddess Frigg.

Tanist: (Celtic) Heir; successor; other self.

Teucer: (Trojan) An archer who fought on the Greek side during the Trojan War.

Thorri: (Icelandic) A spirit of Winter.

Tityas: (Greek) A giant.

Uraeus: (Egyptian) A representation of a serpent's head, usually a cobra. It is worn on the headdresses of pharaohs and deities.

Utnapishtim: (Babylonian) The hero in the story of the flood in the Epic of Gilgamesh. Hebrews based their Noah myth on him.

Veela: (Slavic) A nymph. Veelas are associated with the places they dwell, such as clouds, meadows, oceans, ponds, and trees.

Widdershins: Counterclockwise.

Windigo: (Algonquin) A supernatural creature that eats humans; a spirit that possesses starving people and turns them into monstrous cannibals.

Witch's Ladder: A string of forty beads or a cord of forty knots, into which things such as beads, bones, feathers, sticks, and stones may be knotted. It is used as a talisman, meditation device, or an aid to concentration.

Wortcraft: Herbalism.

Yang: Male energy; the male principle.

Yin: Female energy; the female principle.

🐚 Glossary of Materials

Adam and Eve root: *Orchis mascula*, a rare purple orchid that is also called purple orchis and satyrion. It has tuberous roots, one larger than the other. For magick, the larger root is considered male; the smaller one is considered female.

Adder's tongue: *Erythronium spp.*, low woodland herbs of the northern hemisphere that are also called serpent's tongue, yellow snake-leaf, rattlesnake violet, dog-tooth violet, fawn lily, and trout lily. Adder's tongue has one broad, flat, green leaf and two or three slender stalks with leaves that have yellowish-green spots.

Alexandrite: A variety of chrysoberyl that varies in color from green to red.

Amazonite: A green variety of feldspar.

Amber: Fossilized pine-tree resin.

Ambergris: Sperm whales secrete true ambergris, which is said to smell like a combination of cypress and patchouli. Commercial ambergris is usually an oil blend that mimics this scent.

Apache tear: A translucent black obsidian nodule.

Apatite: A phosphate mineral.

Apophyllite: A class of minerals that is usually white or clear, and tends to flake when heated.

Balm of Gilead: I. *Commiphora gileadensis*, also called Mecca balsam, is a small evergreen Middle Eastern tree that provides resin that can be used for incense. 2. In the West, the fragrant buds of poplar (*Populus candicans*) trees are also called balm of Gilead, and used in magick.

Bat nut: The hard, pointed black seedpod of *Trapa bicornis*, an aquatic plant. It is also called bull's head, devil pod, and water chestnut.

Bdellium: *Commiphora africana*, a small tree of southern Africa. Its bark exudes an aromatic gum that can be burned as incense. It is also called African bdellium, African myrrh, gum bdellium, and hairy corkwood.

Belleric: *Terminalia bellerica*, a tall deciduous tree of Northern India whose dried fruits are used in Ayurvedic medicine. It is also called baehra, kalidruma, karshaphala, vibhitaki, and beleric myrobalan.

Bitter orange: *Citrus aurantium var. amara*, an evergreen citrus tree also called Seville orange, sour orange, and citrus amara. Its flowers yield neroli oil; its seeds and twigs yield petitgrain oil; its fruit yields bitter orange oil.

Bloodroot or blood root: *Sanguinaria canadensis*, a perennial North American herb with scalloped leaves that contains reddish sap. It is also called red root, coon root, red paint root, and red puccoon. ☠

Brimstone: Sulfur, especially when burned over charcoal as incense.

Civet: The musky secretions of small mammals called civets. Once used in perfumery, it has been replaced by synthetic fragrances that mimic its scent.

Datura: *Datura stramonium,* a rank weed that blooms with fragrant white or purple trumpet-shaped flowers, and fruits with a prickly green capsule that resembles that of a horse chestnut. Other names for it include loco-weed, thorn apple, jimson weed or jimsonweed, angel's trumpet, *concombre zombie* (zombie's cucumber), devil's apple, and yerba del diablo (devil's herb). ☠

Deerstongue: *Frasera speciosa,* a vanilla-scented perennial plant of the gentian family. It has whorls of green basal leaves, and blooms with tall spikes of purple-speckled flowers that have four petals. Deerstongue is also called elkweed, deer ears, green gentian, monument plant, wild vanilla, and vanilla leaf.

Dittany of Crete: *Origanum dictamnus,* a perennial herb with grayish-white oval leaves. It is also called Crete dittany, and hop marjoram.

Dragon's blood: A dark-red resin that produces aromatic smoke when burned as incense. Only plants of the *Croton, Daemonorops,* and *Dracena* families produce true dragon's blood.

Electrum: An alloy of gold and silver.

Euphorbia: *Euphorbia spp.,* a large genus of annual or perennial herbs, shrubs, and small trees that produce a milky sap. Euphorbia is also called spurge.

Eye of Satan: *Arbrus precatorius,* a vine that produces red seeds that have black or blue "eyes." It is also called rosary pea, jequirity, red bead vine, lady bug seed, precatory pea, Indian licorice, eye of the ghost, crab's eye vine, and by many other names. ☠

Figwort: *Scrophularia nodosa,* a perennial herb with dark green leaves and knotted roots. Other names for it include throatwort, scrofula plant, rosenoble, cervicaria, kennelwort, stinking Christopher, knotted figwort, and nodding figwort.

Fly agaric: *Amanita muscaria,* a hallucinogenic toadstool whose cap is usually red with white spots. It is also called amanita, spotted toadstool, flycap, pong, and pank. ☠

Fumitory: *Fumaria spp.,* annual flowering weeds that have a whitish bloom on their leaves. The dried leaves can be burned as incense. Other names for fumitory include beggary, smoke, earth smoke, and wax dolls.

Galangal: *Alpinia galanga* or *Alpinia officinalis,* plants of the ginger family with aromatic roots. They are also called chewing John and African juju powder.

Galbanum: A musky gum resin extracted from the stem of *Ferula galbaniflua,* also called *Ferula gummosa.* This perennial herb is native to Iran and blooms with umbels of yellow flowers. Galbanum can be burned as incense.

Gum ammoniac: A gum resin produced by the stems of *Dorema ammoniacum,* a tall perennial plant. It is also called ammoniacum, ammoniac gum, and Persian gum.

Hart's tongue: *Asplenium scolopendrium,* a European fern with simple undivided fronds.

Hartwort: *Tordylium maximum,* a coarse European weed that has serrated leaves and blooms with umbels of white flowers.

Heliodor: A yellow variety of beryl.

Herb Paris: *Paris quadrifolia,* a Eurasian plant that has a whorl of four large green leaves at its base and blooms with threadlike yellowish flowers. It grows in damp, shady places and is also called one-berry, true-love, and true-lover's knot.

Herb Robert: *Geranium robertianum,* a rank, weedy type of geranium.

High John: The bulbous brown root of *Ipomoea purga,* a twining Mexican vine of the morning glory family. It is also called jalup, jalup root, bind-weed, man root, king root, man of the earth, king of the woods, John the Conqueror root, and High John the Conqueror root.

Holy thistle: *Cnicus benedictus,* a thistle-like herb with a reddish branching stem. It is also called blessed thistle.

Jacinth: A variety of zircon that is usually red. It is also called hyacinth.

Kidneywort: *Eupatorium purpureum,* a North American herb with whorled leaves and purple-spotted flowers. It is also called boneset, gravelweed, hempweed, gravel root, joe-pye weed, jopi weed, kidney root, marsh milk-weed, purple boneset, trumpet weed, and queen of the meadow.

Kunzite: A pink variety of the mineral spodumene.

Labdanum: An aromatic resin that can be burned as incense. Mediter-ranean rockrose plants, *Cistus creticus* and *Cistus ladanifer,* provide it.

Loosestrife: *Lythrum salicaria,* a spreading perennial herb that blooms with purplish flowers. Other names for it include purple loosestrife, purple willowherb, and black blood.

Low John: The root of *Trillium grandiflorum,* a perennial woodland herb with whorled leaves that blooms with large white three-petaled flowers. Its many names include great trillium, great white trillium, snow trillium, southern John, wake robin, ground lily, wood lily, birth root, and beth root.

Moonwort: *Lunaria annua,* a biennial herb with translucent papery seed-pods. Other names for it include honesty, silver dollar, moneywort, and money plant.

Motherwort: *Leonuris cardiaca,* a hairy perennial herb that smells like horehound. It is also called lion's tail, lion's ear, chongwei, and cardiaca.

Mouse-eared hawkweed: *Hieracium pilsoella,* a creeping plant that is also called St. John's flower, and St. John's blood.

Neroli: (see Bitter Orange)

Olibanum: *Boswellia serrata,* an aromatic gum resin that is so similar to frankincense that the two words are generally used interchangeably. Like frankincense, it is burned as incense.

Opoponax: The gum resin of *Commiphora holtziana,* an African tree.

Orache: *Atriplex patula,* a North American weed that grows on alkaline or salty soil and blooms with small white flowers that have three petals. It is also called arrach, spearscale, common orache, spear orach, spear saltbush, and spreading orache.

Orris root: The aromatic root of any of several types of iris: *Iris florentina, Iris germanica,* and *Iris pallida.* It is also called Queen Elizabeth root.

Pipestone: Red claystone, a variety of limestone that is found in clay deposits. Also called catlinite, it was used by Native Americans to carve pipes.

Queen of the night: *Selenicereus grandiflora,* a night-blooming cactus that is also called Moon cereus, and reina de la noche. Night-blooming varieties of *Cereus,* as well as other varieties of *Selenicereus,* are also called by these names.

Rubellite: A reddish variety of tourmaline.

Savin: *Juniperus savina,* a small ornamental evergreen Eurasian shrub with needlelike leaves. It is also called savin juniper.

Scammony: *Convolvulus scammonia,* a twining perennial Eurasian vine of the morning glory family. Also called Syrian bindweed, it has arrow-shaped leaves and blooms with yellow flowers.

Scorpion-grass: *Myosotis stricta,* a short annual herb of the borage family that blooms with tiny light blue flowers. Other names for it include blue scorpion grass, small-flowered forget-me-not, and upright forget-me-not.

Scorpion weed: *Phacelia spp.,* a large genus of annual North American herbs. Many bloom with purple flowers. Other names for them include California bluebell, desert bluebell, purple phacelia, purple scorpionweed, shade scorpion-weed, and wild heliotrope.

Scullcap: *Scutellaria galericulata,* a small European shrub that blooms with blue flowers. Other names for it include hoodwort, madweed, mad dogwood, and blue pimpernel.

Shower of gold: *Cassia fistula,* an ornamental tropical tree that blooms with long hanging clusters of bright yellow flowers. It is also called yellow shower, golden shower tree, golden rain, Indian laburnum, drumstick tree, purging cassia, and pudding pipe tree.

Silverweed: *Potentilla anserina,* a creeping plant with silvery hairs on its leaves. Its many names include wild tansy, prince's feathers, trailing tansy, wild agrimony, goosewort, silvery cinquefoil, goose tansy, traveler's joy, moor grass, and wild agrimony.

Smartweed: *Polygonum hydropiper,* an annual wetland plant with reddish stems and greenish flowers. It is also called water pepper, marsh pepper, lake weed, sickleweed, biting knotweed, and bloodwort.

Smithsonite: Zinc carbonate, a mineral ore of zinc that is also called zinc spar.

Spignel: *Meum athamanticum,* an aromatic perennial northern European plant that has dark green feathery leaves, blooms with umbels of tiny flowers, and produces seeds that smell like curry. Other names for it include alpine fennel, baldmoney, bearwort, meu or mew, and spicknel.

Spikenard: *Nardostachys grandiflora,* a flowering Asian plant of the valerian family. Its root yields an aromatic essential oil that can be burned as incense. Spikenard is also called nard, nardin, and musk root.

Storax: *Styrax officinalis,* an evergreen Eurasian shrub or small tree whose aromatic wood can be burned as incense. It is also called snowbell, styrax, and snowdrop bush.

Sunstone*:* A sparkling variety of feldspar.

Sulphurwort: *Peucedanum officinale,* a European salt marsh plant that resembles fennel. It blooms with umbels of tiny flowers and has a thick taproot that smells like sulfur. Other names for it include brimstonewort, chucklusa, hoar strange, hoar strong, hog's fennel, milk parsley, marsh parsley, marsh smallage, sow fennel, and sulphur weed.

Ti: *Cordyline terminalis,* an evergreen tropical perennial plant with leaves that vary in color from pink to intense red. It is also called Hawaiian good luck plant.

Uva ursi: *Arctostaphylos uva ursi,* a low trailing evergreen shrub whose fruit is a bright red berry. Other names for it include bearberry, bear's grape, crow berry, fox berry, and hog cranberry.

Witch grass or witchgrass: *Panicum capillare,* an annual North American grass. It is also called mousseline, hair grass, panic grass, tickle grass, tumble grass, and old witch grass.

Wolfbane: *Aconitum napellus,* a tall perennial herb with dark green leaves and a fleshy taproot. It is also called aconite, monkshood, Thor's hat, and by other names. ☠

Wood aloes: *Aquilaria sinensis,* an evergreen tree whose bark yields an aromatic resin. It is also called aloeswood, aquilaria, eagle wood, incense tree, Chinese incense tree, heung tree, lignum aloes, and chen xiang.

Selected Bibliography

Andrews, Ted. *Animal Speak: The Spiritual and Magical Powers of Creatures Great and Small.* St. Paul, MN: Llewellyn Publications, 2003.

————. *Animal Wise: The Spirit Language and Signs of Nature.* Jacksonville, TN: Dragonhawk Publishing, 1999.

Aristotle (attributed to). *Secretum Secretorum.* Sami Salman al-A'War, trans. Beirut: Dar al-'Arabiyah lil-Tibaàh, 1995.

Barrett, Francis. *The Magus, or Celestial Intelligencer; Being a Complete System of Occult Philosophy in Three Books.* London: Lackington, Alley, & Co., 1801: Reprinted York Beach, ME: Samuel Weiser, 1999.

Best, Michael R., and Frank H. Brightman. *The Book of Secrets of Albertus Magnus of the Virtues of Herbs, Stones and Certain Beasts.* York Beach, ME: Samuel Weiser, 1999.

Betz, Hans Deiter, ed. *The Greek Magical Papyri in Translation, Including the Demotic Spells.* Chicago: University of Chicago Press, 1992.

Bowker, John, ed. *The Oxford Dictionary of World Religions.* New York: Oxford University Press, 1997.

Bulfinch, Thomas. *Bulfinch's Mythology.* New York: Modern Library, 1988.

Burriss, Eli Edward. *Taboo, Magic, Spirits: A Study of Primitive Elements in Roman Religion.* New York: MacMillan Company, 1931.

Campbell, Joseph. *The Masks of God* (4 volumes). New York: Viking Press, 1975.

Cotterell, Arthur. *A Dictionary of World Mythology.* New York: Oxford University Press, 1990.

————. *The Encyclopedia of Mythology.* New York: Southmark, 1996.

Couzens, Reginald C. *The Stories of the Months and Days.* New York: Frederick A. Stokes Co., 1923.

Culpepper Nicholas. *Culpepper's Complete Herbal and English Physician.* Glenwood, IL: Meyerbooks, 1990.

Cunningham, Scott. *Cunningham's Encyclopedia of Magical Herbs.* St. Paul, MN: Llewellyn Publications, 1999.

Davidson, Gustav. *A Dictionary of Angels: Including the Fallen Angels.* New York: The Free Press, 1967.

Farrar, Janet and Stewart. *A Witches' Bible.* Custer, WA: Phoenix Publishing, 1996.

Fernie, William T., M.D. *Precious Stones: For Curative Wear, Other Remedial Uses and Likewise the Nobler Metals.* Kila, MT: Kessinger Publications, LLC.

Fischer-Schreiber, Ingrid, et al. *The Encyclopedia of Eastern Philosophy and Religion.* Boston: Shambhala, 1994.

Folkard, Richard. *Plant Lore, Legends and Lyrics: Myths, Traditions, Superstitions, and Folk-lore of the Plant Kingdom.* London: Sampson Low, Marston & Company, Ltd., 1892.

Frazer, Sir James G. *The Golden Bough: A Study in Magic and Religion.* New York: The MacMillan Company, 1953.

Gimbutas, Marija. *The Living Goddesses.* Berkeley: University of California Press, 1999.

Goodrich, Norma Lorre. *Ancient Myths.* New York: Meridien Books, 1994.

Grant, Michael, and John Litzel. *Who's Who—Classical Mythology.* Routledge Who's Who Series. London: Routledge, 1995.

Graves, Robert. *The Greek Myths, Volumes I and II.* Baltimore: Penguin Books, 1955.

———. *The White Goddess.* New York: Farrar, Straus and Giroux, 1966.

Hamilton, Edith. *Mythology.* Boston: Little, Brown and Company, 1942.

Holland, Eileen. *Holland's Grimoire of Magickal Correspondences.* Franklin Lakes, NJ: New Page, 2005.

———. *The Wicca Handbook.* York Beach, ME: Samuel Weiser, 2000.

Jordan, Michael. *Encyclopedia of Gods.* New York: Facts on File, 1993.

Kightly, Charles. *The Perpetual Almanack of Folklore.* New York: Thames and Hudson, 1987.

Knight, Richard Payne. *The Symbolical Language of Ancient Art and Mythology.* New York: J. W. Houghton, 1876.

Lewis, James R., and Evelyn Dorothy Oliver. *Angels A to Z.* New York: Gale Research, 1996.

Lilley, William. *Christian Astrology, 1647.* New York: Astrology Classics, 2005.

MacCulloch, John Arnott. *The Religion of the Ancient Celts.* Edinburgh: T. & T. Clark, 1911.

Monaghan, Patricia. *The Book of Goddesses and Heroines.* New York: E. P. Dutton, 1981.

Oliver, Lewis. *Angels A to Z.* Detroit: Visible Ink Press, 1983.

Osborn, Harold. *South American Mythology.* New York: Peter Bedrick Books, 1986.

Rosenberg, Donna. *World Mythology: An Anthology of the Great Myths and Legends.* Lincolnwood, IL: NTC Publishing Group, 1993.

Sargent, Denny. *Global Ritualism: Myth and Magic around the World.* St. Paul, MN: Llewellyn Publications, 1994.

Shearer, Alastair. *The Hindu Vision: Forms of the Formless.* New York: Thames & Hudson, 1993.

Spence, Lewis. *An Encyclopaedia of Occultism.* Secaucus, NJ: Citadel Press, 1993.

Starhawk (Miriam Simos). *The Spiral Dance: A Rebirth of the Ancient Religion of the Great Goddess.* San Francisco: HarperSanFrancisco, 1989.

Sykes, Egerton. *Who's Who: Non-Classical Mythology.* New York: Oxford University Press, 1993.

Turner, Patricia, and Charles Russell Coulter. *Dictionary of Ancient Deities.* New York: Oxford University Press, 2000.

Von Nettesheim, and Heinrich Cornelius Agrippa. *Three Books of Occult Philosophy.* London: Gregory Moule, 1651.

Watterson, Barbara. *The Gods of Ancient Egypt.* London: B. T. Batsford, 1984.

Weiser, Francis X. *Handbook of Christian Feasts and Customs.* New York: Harcourt, Brace and World, Inc., 1958.

About the Author

Eileen Holland is a Wiccan priestess, a solitary eclectic witch who calls her path Goddess Wicca. Author of several books about magick and witchcraft, she is also webmaster of Open, Sesame (*www.open-sesame.com*), a long-running Wiccan website that has had millions of visitors. Eileen lives quietly in upstate New York, where she continuess to study and write about things that interest her: ethnobotany, magick, mythology, and witchcraft.